the early work

LOUISE **BOURGEOIS**

LOUISE BOURGEOIS

the early work

by Josef Helfenstein

KRANNERT ART MUSEUM
University of Illinois at Urbana-Champaign

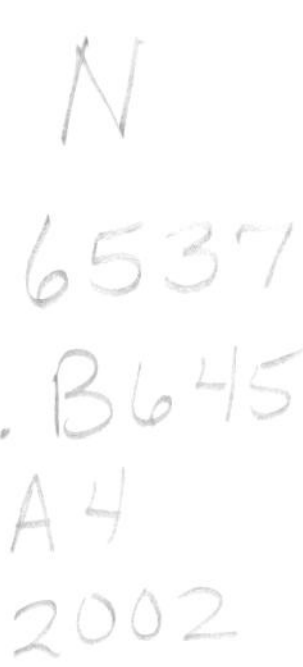

This book serves as the catalogue for the exhibition,
Louise Bourgeois: The Early Work, organized by Krannert Art Museum.

On the cover: Louise Bourgeois' Personages *on exhibit at Peridot Gallery in New York City, 1950. (Photography: H. Messer, front cover, and Aaron Siskind, back cover)*

CONCEPT: Josef Helfenstein, Director, Krannert Art Museum
CURATORIAL ASSISTANCE: Sarah Eckhardt and Natasha Ritsma
PROJECT COORDINATORS: Karen Hewitt and Sarah Eckhardt
PRODUCTION ASSISTANCE: Rhonda Bruce, Paula McCarty, Kerry Morgan, and Cynthia Voelkl
DESIGN: Evelyn C. Shapiro

© Louise Bourgeois for all illustrations of her work.
© 2002 by The Board of Trustees of the University of Illinois. All rights reserved.

Library of Congress Number 2002105079
ISBN 0-295-98248-9

Distributed by University of Washington Press
Manufactured in Canada

KRANNERT ART MUSEUM · 500 East Peabody Drive · Champaign, Illinois 61820 USA

LENDERS TO THE EXHIBITION

Louise Bourgeois, courtesy of Cheim & Read
Jerry Gorovoy
Ginny Williams
Peter Blum Gallery
The Art Collection of Bank One
Whitney Museum of American Art

EXHIBITION SCHEDULE

Krannert Art Museum, University of Illinois at Urbana-Champaign
May 1 – August 4, 2002

Madison Art Center, Madison, Wisconsin
September 15 – November 17, 2002

Aspen Art Museum, Aspen, Colorado
December 13, 2002 – February 2, 2003

FUNDERS TO THE EXHIBITION

Krannert Art Museum Council
Flex-N-Gate
Prairie Gardens
Alice and John Pfeffer
Illinois Arts Council

LONGWOOD UNIVERSITY LIBRARY
REDFORD AND RACE STREET
FARMVILLE, VA 23909

CONTENTS

preface

THIS BOOK AND THE EXHIBITION IT ACCOMPANIES are the result of my interest in the work of this outstanding artist that began almost two decades earlier. After encountering the work of Louise Bourgeois on different occasions in Europe and the United States, I finally had the privilege to meet the artist in New York in the fall of 1989. Through her generosity and the continuous support of her assistant, Jerry Gorovoy, and with the cooperation of my former colleagues in Bern, Switzerland, in 1991 the Kunstmuseum Bern was a venue for the first European retrospective of the work of Louise Bourgeois. That exhibition, organized by Peter Weiermair in Frankfurt, provided the impetus for the Kunstmuseum Bern to begin collecting Bourgeois' work, with a special focus on her drawings. With almost thirty drawings from the 1940s until the most recent years, the Kunstmuseum Bern owns one of the finest public collections of her works on paper.

The work of Louise Bourgeois has been celebrated throughout the world in the last fifteen years. Beginning in the 1940s, shortly after moving to New York City, Bourgeois produced her first mature, highly original works. Her pieces were included in several group exhibitions with the Abstract Expressionists, such as Willem De Kooning, Robert Motherwell and Jackson Pollock, and she was associated with many avant-garde artists in New York, including exiled European Surrealists and Dadaists. Born in Paris in 1911, Bourgeois is among the very few living representatives of that generation and she is still actively involved in the international art scene.

Krannert Art Museum is proud and deeply honored to organize the exhibition *Louise Bourgeois: The Early Work*, the most comprehensive display of her early work since Deborah Wye's groundbreaking retrospective at the Museum of Modern Art in New York in 1982. In 1994 the St. Louis Art Museum organized *The Personages*, the first museum exhibition ever devoted exclusively to Bourgeois' early sculpture. *Louise Bourgeois: The Early Work* displays more than eighty sculptures, paintings, drawings, and prints. Some of the works have never been shown before in public.

While most of her contemporaries were drawn toward pure abstraction, the work of Louise Bourgeois entered the realm of the psychological and symbolic. Themes already evident in these early works continued to resonate throughout her career. The *Personages* represent her first explorations in sculpture; summoning a physical presence, they suggest moments of alienation as well as evocative encounters. The fifteen psychologically charged paintings included in this exhibition are examples of Bourgeois' brief exploration with painting. Several of her paintings and drawings depict a woman's identity physically merging with architecture and the domestic space, implying a frightening outcome. The subject matter for the drawings varies from landscapes of Bourgeois' childhood and anthropomorphic houses to alienating machines and high-rise buildings. The series of prints, *He Disappeared into Complete Silence* (1947), inspired by New York's landscape of skyscrapers, reflects her experiences of moving from Europe to metropolitan America, presenting her own hermetic texts juxtaposed with enigmatic pictures.

Our profound thanks go to the lenders of the exhibition, both private and public. We are indebted to the following institutions and individuals for providing these loans: Lisa Erf, Curator, and John Dodge, Registrar, for Bank One Art Program, Chicago; Ginny Williams, and her assistant, Barbara Wathke, from the Ginny Williams Family Foundation, Denver; Peter Blum and Liorah Gardiner, of Peter Blum Gallery, New York; John Cheim, Director of the Cheim & Read Gallery, New York; Jerry Gorovoy, Assistant, and Wendy Williams, Managing Director, of the Louise Bourgeois Studio. We are especially grateful to Louise Bourgeois since the artist has lent by far the largest portion of the exhibition.

I am very grateful to Jonathan Fineberg, Professor in the art history program at the University of Illinois at Urbana-Champaign, for his assistance in contacting colleagues as possible venues for this exhibition. I also thank Dean Sobel, Director, Aspen Art Museum, for his advice and support, and Sarah Krajewsky, Curator, and Stephen Fleischman, Director, of the Madison Art Center.

This exhibition was possible only through the hard work of the members of Krannert Art Museum staff. I especially thank Sarah Eckhardt, Curatorial Assistant, for her commitment. Sarah was instrumental in organizing the exhibition and in preparing and coordinating the publication of the catalogue. She provided research assistance for the essay and coordinated the programs related to the show. Natasha Ritsma provided additional research and assistance. Karen Hewitt, Associate Director, was crucial in overseeing and coordinating the many aspects related to the publication as well as the exhibition and its venues. Cynthia Voelkl, Assistant to the Director, and Paula McCarty, managed correspondence and exhibition coordination. Kathleen Jones, Registrar, was instrumental in coordinating loans and organizing the exhibition. Diane Schumacher, Assistant to the Director for Public Relations and Special Services, coordinated events and programs and was responsible for public relations work. Ann Rasmus, Education Director, helped with programming and organizing guided tours. Kerry Morgan, Curator, and Rhonda Bruce, Department Secretary, helped review and prepare the final manuscript. Eric Lemme, Exhibits Designer, and Lisa Costello, Exhibits Preparator, provided indispensable assistance in mounting the exhibition along with Nathan Westerman and John Cichon. Last but certainly not least, I thank Evelyn C. Shapiro, for the design and development of the catalogue and for a very productive collaboration.

For generously sharing their knowledge and enthusiasm in creating programs related to the exhibition, I am indebted to Jordana Mendelson, Assistant Professor of Art History, and to Kal Alston, Director, and Jacque Kahn, Associate Director, of the Women's Studies Program at the University of Illinois at Urbana-Champaign. Together, these colleagues organized an interdisciplinary colloquium on Louise Bourgeois in conjunction with the Women's Studies larger spring series, "Women and Creativity."

But our deepest thanks go to Louise Bourgeois. It has always been a unique pleasure and a real privilege to spend time and to work with her. Our warmest thanks go to Jerry Gorovoy and to Wendy Williams for their generous assistance and advice. Without their support, and the help of John Cheim, this outstanding exhibition would not have been possible.

BETWEEN RITUAL AND REPRESENTATION

The Early Work of Louise Bourgeois

THE EARLY PAINTINGS, DRAWINGS, AND SCULPTURES of Louise Bourgeois are imbued with a breadth and complexity of forms and meanings. Underlying her early work is an unprecedented expression of the existential situation of woman in modern western society and a profoundly personal exploration of the fundamental role the family plays in personal development. Bourgeois persistently delves into her own biography in her early work, drawing upon decisive moments before and after her arrival in the United States in 1938. In ways that are sometimes obvious and other times veiled and ambiguous the artist alludes to biological, emotional, and societal issues that affect women, and investigates in an almost anthropological way the origins of family, political constraints, and basic instincts and forms of behavior.

Between 1945 and 1955, Bourgeois made approximately eighty sculptures. The *Personages* were originally executed in wood, but the artist always intended to cast them in bronze. Their translation into bronze began in 1959 and has been finished only recently.[1] The making of the *Personages* coincided with an intense period in her life as mother and wife with a young family of three children, surrounded by an almost exclusively masculine group of Abstract Expressionist painters who thought of David Smith as their representative sculptor.

One of the motivating factors for Bourgeois to leave painting and begin working with sculpture was the greater physical impact conveyed by this medium. Physical tangibility was indispensable for her to express emotional intensity.[2] Based on memories of her childhood in France and on her experiences in New York in the 1940s and early 1950s, the *Personages* deal with a highly personal and complex range of physical and emotional conditions: growth and maternal symbols in conjunction with nature (*Spring, Breasted Woman*), fertility as an expression of physical vulnerability (*Pregnant Woman*); the instrumentalization of the female body in a patriarchal society (*Paddle Woman, Spoon Woman, Needle Woman, Woman in the Shape of a Shuttle*); the symbolic combination of body and architecture (*Pillar*), an ambivalent commentary on the role of women in western society; depression and alienation as an existential experience (*Depression Woman*); aggression, hostility and opposition (*Persistent Antagonism, Knife Couple, Dagger Child*); exorcism of physical violence (*Portrait of C.Y.*); exhibitionism and sexual dependence, expressed in mythological terms (*The Three Graces*); distance and immobility (*Sleeping Figure, Observer*); exclusion and the forced passiveness of physical isolation (*Quarantania*); the utopia of escape (*Winged Figure*); dependence, dominance and one-sided communication

(*The Listening One*, *Brother and Sister*); deception and helplessness (*The Blind Leading the Blind*); and death and the exorcism of fear of death (*The Tomb of a Young Person*).

The *Personages*, the most distinct group of work in the early years, have only recently been recognized as an outstanding and highly complex contribution to the history of sculpture in the twentieth century. Although Bourgeois has developed her work in unprecedented directions after 1955 until this very moment, constantly shifting to new concepts, styles and materials, the *Personages* provide the key to the crucial themes and concerns of her entire body of work.

ART OR ARTIFACT—FREUD'S TOYS

In the late 1980s, Bourgeois wrote an essay on Sigmund Freud as a collector, in which she analyzed the relationship between the psychoanalyst and the art objects—mostly from ancient Egypt, classical Greece and Rome, and ancient China—with which he surrounded himself. The essay, written in Bourgeois' clear-cut, brilliantly definite prose, was published in Artforum in 1990.[3] The text provides an interesting perspective on Bourgeois' understanding of Freud and her perception of meanings attached to cultural objects in a private context. Bourgeois focuses on the role and function of Freud's collection in his daily life, and approaches the topic from her personal and anthropological, rather than purely artistic interest in the topic. Freud, Bourgeois stated categorically, "was not a visual person, his collection has no visual consistency." Instead, Bourgeois analyzes the psychological and intellectual relationship between Freud and his objects. With underlying sarcasm, Bourgeois noted that Freud was only interested in the past: "He could hold the antiquities, he could caress them, he could dust them, he could handle them physically." But the artist did not believe Freud had a genuine cultural interest of an instinctual feeling for the artistic qualities of the objects he collected: "These objects were not crucial to Freud's work. They were his toys. They gave him a kick. They were part of the good life, and as I said, he may have needed reassurance.... As a healer, Freud was a very powerful person. Meaning that reality for him was not in the little figures."

Assuming the role of analyst herself, Bourgeois reflected on the role of his parents for Freud as a collector: "We all want to defend our parents. It was when Freud's father died that he started to collect, and in his collecting he was very generous. He accepted all these figures. He gave a place to every one of them, so therefore *he* had a place, too. Their being there on the desk or on his shelf was a physical thing." Comparing the function of collecting artworks for Freud to the role of the pebbles collected by her father, Bourgeois acknowledged that ownership of objects, either artworks or artifacts, has an existential meaning: "Both [a Greek statue or a pebble] can help you to believe that life has an order and a raison d'être."

At this point in the essay, Bourgeois recognized her argument was somewhat contradictory. After initially stating that Freud's collection reflected societal values more than a genuine personal interest in the art, Bourgeois then explained the difference between an artifact and a work of art: "An artifact is first of all useful, and does not relate to anything

FIGURES 1–2 *Louise Bourgeois, circa 1944, on the roof of her apartment building, 142 East 18th Street, New York City.*

more vitally than to its use. It is isolated in its momentary meaning, and is easily reproduced. It is not an original." Returning to her initial judgment regarding the lack of artistic quality in Freud's collection, Bourgeois concludes that his objects cannot serve as personal symbols or as symbols of their time. She summarizes by describing his collections as toys: "A toy is fine, but it's only a toy. It's not a reality. Art is a reality."

For Bourgeois, the ultimate distinction between "toys" (artifacts) and art is the existential involvement of the maker. Art is a personal symbol, and exactly this is its ultimate function, since for Bourgeois art is always the result of a process of pain and suffering that no analysis can solve. "To be an artist involves some suffering. That's why artists repeat themselves—because they have no access to a cure."

Bourgeois' essay on Freud is a decidedly personal statement and in many ways a very instructive summary of some of her most essential convictions as an artist. The text provides especially interesting insights into Bourgeois' concepts and feelings about the role of art and the physical and existential relation between the artist and the objects she or he creates. Although written in a seemingly rigid and uncompromising style, her language includes a strong portion of irony and parody in contract to the seriousness of her subject.

THE MAKING OF THE *PERSONAGES*—THE TABULA RASA OF THE ROOF

In the summer of 1941, Louise Bourgeois and her husband, Robert Goldwater, rented an apartment on 142 East 18th Street in Manhattan. The building, called Stuyvesant's Folly, was the oldest apartment house in New York. They had two sons, Michel Olivier, born in

1936, whom they had adopted in 1939, and Jean-Louis, born in the summer of 1940. When they moved to their new apartment, Bourgeois was pregnant with her third son Alain, who was born in November 1941. The family lived on 18th Street until 1958. Bourgeois painted in the studio of the apartment and began using the roof of the building as an open air studio as well. In 1941, Goldwater and Bourgeois also acquired a summer house in Easton, Connecticut.

It was soon after 1941 when Bourgeois started to work on a new group of standing wood figures which she would later call *Personages*. During this creative time, the roof of her house in Manhattan became an important location to develop and to test her work. On the one side, the roof provided an escape from the apartment and the never-ending daily obligations as mother and wife. But more than that, working on the roof lifted the artist into a completely neutral environment, devoid of any sign of claustrophobic encroachment.

The space on the roof, open to the surrounding architecture as well as to the sky, was part of the urban landscape. As an empty spot, it seemed purely functional, with no superfluous decoration to affect its stark neutrality. At the same time, the roof offered the liberating experience of the immeasurable open sky.† The cyclic movement of the sun with its changing patterns of shadow was the only movement affecting the neutral environment.

A series of photographs from the mid-1940s show Bourgeois on the roof of the apartment building during the time when she worked on the *Personages*. In two of the photos Bourgeois appears at the same spot, seen from the front (fig. 1) and from the back (fig. 2). Bourgeois wears working clothes, but there are no traces of her work. Strong light

†See Bourgeois' text from 1947 "The Puritan," an homage to the New York sky: "Do you know the New York sky? You should, it is supposed to be known. It is outstanding. It is a serious thing. Can you remember the Paris sky? How unreliable, most of the time gray, often warm and damp, never quite perfect, indulging in clouds and shades; rain, breeze, and sun sometimes managing to appear together. But the New York sky is blue, utterly blue. The light is white, a glorying white and the air is strong and it is healthy too. There is no foolishness about that sky. It is a beautiful thing. It is pure."[4]

FIGURES 3–4
Louise Bourgeois, circa 1944, on the roof of her apartment building, 142 East 18th Street, New York City.

permeates the surface of the roof creating sharp contrasts and a geometric pattern of bright and dark areas that emphasize the emptiness and rawness of the urban zone.

In another photograph, Bourgeois is seen from below, leaning over the edge of the roof (fig. 3). Her silhouette is detached from an overwhelmingly clear sky. Another image (fig. 4) is dominated by the view of the architectural landscape on 18th Street, offering additional views of the lower facades in the close neighborhood; despite the view downwards into the street channels, no other person is visible. Bourgeois, her face smiling, seems to be at ease in confronting the overwhelming density of the surrounding high-rise buildings.

There exists only one photo with Bourgeois next to her sculptures on the roof (fig. 5). It is a group of seven thin, tall wood sculptures, painted in white. They are standing next to each other, some rising in straight verticality, others slightly oblique. Three of them have small wood pieces staked on top. There are no traces of surface carving. Bourgeois stands on the right in front of the sculptures, smiling, her hands in a gesture of suspended movement. The *Personages* behind her seem to rise into the sky. The photograph, taken from about the height of Bourgeois' hands, shows only the upper part of the sculptures, echoing the impression of an architectural skyline. The image does not convey how the sculptures were fixed on the floor in order to stand on their own. The neutralizing effect of the sunlight emphasizes the simplified forms of the sculptures, their flat surfaces and similarity to skyscrapers.

Another photo from approximately the same time shows Bourgeois in a narrow space on top of the stairs under the roof of her house, standing behind a similar or the same group of standing figures (fig. 6). The narrative title of this group of *Personages,* "The Visitors Arrive at the Doors,"[5] evokes figures of the past. The photo indicates an orchestrated scene with Bourgeois emerging from a dark background, as if she had just opened a door to greet

the sculptures. Her face and right hand, dramatically illuminated, relate to the bright areas of the sculptures in the foreground. Despite the poor quality, the photograph seems to reveal a strong, almost mysterious connection between the artist and her work.

The display of the *Personages* on the roof situates them not only in a metaphorical, but also in a physical relationship with the urban environment. The sculptures are in fact made of the same wood as that used to construct the water towers on top of the buildings in Manhattan.[6] But in addition, the photographs of Louise Bourgeois on the roof strikingly document the significance of an essential theme in her work, the analogy between human figure and architecture. The experience of working on the roof, the visual rawness and functional beauty of this unique landscape of skyscrapers must have had a deep impact on her work. The environment definitely played a role in the creation of the *Personages*, as Bourgeois stated: "Suddenly I had this huge sky space to myself and I began doing these standing figures."[7] The skyscraper, the modernist expansion of the house of the nineteenth century, was the opposite of the over-decorated and over-furnished middle and upper class houses in France where Bourgeois had grown up. After her cultural displacement and arrival in New York, the environment of the skyscrapers—symbol of the economic growth and the strive for supremacy of the New World—provided the ideal environment for expressing her need for independence and emancipation from France and her family. The roof provided the tabula rasa to get rid of the burden of the past.

SCULPTURE AS DOMESTIC OBJECT

The *Personages* reflect not only the forms of the surrounding skyscrapers and therefore the vocabulary of Modernism, but the meaning and content of the sculptures was first and foremost related to people that Bourgeois had left behind in France or met in her new

environment in America. In the artist's own words, the figures "were conceived of and functioned as figures, each given a personality by its shape and articulation, and responding to one another. They were life-size in a real space and made to be seen in groups."[8] Bourgeois was also interested to test her sculptures in environments other than the urban landscape. In several photographs the *Personages* appear either in front of or next to the family's country house in Easton, Connecticut, a scenery that seems more connected to the places she had spent her childhood in France. In figure 7, seven of the *Personages* in progress are lined up against the wall. *Observer* on the right, nearly finished, is the only freestanding figure, planted between rocks on the floor. Of the six figures leaning against the wall, three, among them an early version of *Friendly Evidence* on the right, are painted at least partly in dark color, similar to the painted wall behind them. The bright figure with the small appendage on top (third from the right) later became part of *Quarantania* (page 85). In a photograph from the same period (fig. 8), *Observer* is leaning against the wall with its left arm detached from the body, further emphasizing the impression of the representational animism of these sculptures.

FIGURES 5–6

Opposite page: Louise Bourgeois working on her sculptures on the roof of her apartment building, circa 1944.

Above: Bourgeois in the attic of her apartment building on 142 East 18th Street, circa 1946.

Another document from the same time with Bourgeois and her three sons in front of her, holding hands while standing next to each other (fig. 9), appears strikingly similar to the *Personages* leaned against the wall of the same house. The boys are dressed the same way, with naked torsos. Bourgeois touches the shoulder of Alain, her youngest son, with her hand. Back in the right, Robert Goldwater looks thoughtful while talking to a guest, the painter Charles Prendergast. A photograph from approximately 1948 reveals the interrelationship between sculpture and family members in an even more striking way. Bourgeois' son Jean-Louis poses against the wall of the country house right next to the sculpture *Spring* (fig. 10). The wood figure seems to lean into the human body, the animal in the hands of Jean-Louis adds even more to the blurring of the boundaries between intimate family scene, living bodies, and animated wood sculpture.[9]

Bourgeois, who in general resists talking about her private life in conjunction with her work, nevertheless occasionally touched upon the subtle relationship between the individual idiosyncrasies of the members of her family and the evolution of her work. This seems to be especially true with the *Personages*, when psychic issues in the life of the artist and her family resulted in important shifts: "The monoliths are absolutely stiff—the stiffness of

FIGURES 7–9

At the country house in Easton, Connecticut, circa 1945.

Above, left: *Sculptures in progress.*

Above, right: Observer.

Left: Louise Bourgeois with her three sons, Alain, Jean-Louis, and Michel. Charles Prendergast and Robert Goldwater (right) are in the background.

someone who's afraid. The way one can say, 'he's scared stiff'. Immobilized with fear. Stuck. This was an entire period. And then suddenly there's a kind of softening that came from the softness of my children and of my husband; that changed me a little. I got the nerve to look around me, to let go. Not to be so nervous. Not to be so tense. The pilings make it possible to turn around."[10] With the "gradual change from rigidity to pliability,"[11] from immobility to movement, Bourgeois referred to the second group of *Personages* starting in the 1950s, the segmented pieces (see fig. 22).

FIGURE 10
Louise Bourgeois' son Jean-Louis with cat and Spring, *circa 1948.*

Carrying the sculptures around or placing them in new environments seems to have been an important part of creating them. Bourgeois even carved hand holes in order to improve their capacity to be manipulated easily (fig. 11).[12] By integrating them in the settings with her family, Bourgeois added an animistic dimension to her private domain. The figures charged the space in which they were placed. By manipulating and testing the *Personages* in different settings, the artist changed both the meaning of the sculptures as well as the character of her environment.

The lack of a firm basis on the floor predisposed the way the sculptures had to be handled: unable to stand on their own, the *Personages* had to be either carried around frequently or to be put away and stored in a more permanent way. Bourgeois used to store and display the sculptures in the dumbwaiter of her apartment. The *Personages* denied the usual restrictions imposed by artwork and demanded to be treated like artifacts. By integrating them into her daily life and moving them back and forth from one private environment to another, Bourgeois brought them closer to life, appropriating them as her personal objects. Although working as an artist was an escape from the family obligations, Bourgeois wasn't going to respect the boundaries between art and household. The sculptures were not kept in the neutral space of the studio; by making them part of the family space, they overcame the division between art and life.

The number of photographs documenting the evolution of the *Personages* and their display in different settings is striking and interesting in itself. Several photos show the sculptures displayed in dense proximity or stored in her apartment studio in New York. In figure 12, early versions of *Breasted Woman* and of *Pregnant Woman*, wrapped in cloth, stand in a precarious balance on their own, additional figures lean against the wall. The sculptures seem to have been placed casually, but their closeness enhances the presence of each other, as if they would be ready to interact. The wall is covered with Bourgeois' notes in French and English, adding to the impression of a strange dialogue between the sculptures and their maker (fig. 13). Another photo conveys an even stronger impression

FIGURE 11 Brother and Sister (1949), *with Louise Bourgeois' hands, circa 1980.*

of the powerful and mysterious presence of the sculptures (fig. 14). The group consists of eight figures, among them versions in progress of (from the right) *Observer, Dagger Child, Pillar, Portrait of C.Y., Friendly Evidence* (in the dark, barely recognizable), and a four leg structure that seems to be an early version of *The Blind Leading the Blind*. The photo is taken from a low point, creating the illusion that the figures are all bending their upper part toward a virtual center, as if engaged in a mysterious dialogue. The lighting from below creates dramatic shadows on the wall, reinforcing the animistic presence of the figures and softening the boundaries between physical reality and imagination.

In another photo, probably from 1950 or 1951, the *Personages* appear stored against the wall of Bourgeois' studio (fig. 15). Similar to the document showing the sculptures leaning against the wall of the country house (fig. 7), here the image underscores the quantity and passive character of the figures as objects. Their immobility and mute character reflect states of indifference and self-absorption. Stored like household objects in a closet, the sculptures have to be manipulated in order to be activated. The photograph conveys another important conceptual element of the work: the one-sided relationship between the objects and the artist; they depend on her, she controls them, only she can bring them to life. It is as late as 1975 that we find Bourgeois next to the *Personages*, lined up against the wall of her studio in Brooklyn, engaged in a silent dialogue with her sculptures (fig. 16).

At the same time, the question of a steady platform for the *Personages* became unavoidable. Bourgeois always intended the figures to arise from the floor. The ultimate goal was to make them able to stand on their own. In order to achieve that, they had to be fixed at the most fragile point, since most of the *Personages* come down to one or two narrow points at bottom. The precarious balance, the constant threat of falling over, became inherent to their structure as well as to their meaning. It wasn't until Bourgeois began casting the bronzes that she arrived at a compromise solution of a minimal base. She then similarly mounted the wooden sculptures allowing her to integrate the *Personages* in wood and in bronze in the same installation.

QUARANTANIA

As the photographs documenting the evolution of the *Personages* and their function in relation to the artist reveal, many pieces were developed and reworked over a number of years. Undoing and redoing reflected psychological states in which meanings were not fixed but constantly changing and fundamentally ambiguous. Given its history and content, *Quarantania* is an especially complex sculpture and in many ways a summary of Bourgeois' work on the first group of the *Personages*, the monolithic figures. The five vertical sculptures were first conceived independently and exhibited in the first show at the Peridot Gallery in 1949. In 1953, after at least six years working on them, Bourgeois decided to bring them together permanently and fixed them on a common base (fig. 17). The

FIGURES 12–13
Left: Sculptures in progress at the studio in New York, circa 1945. From left: Breasted Woman, Black Flames, Pregnant Woman *and unidentified sculptures.*

Right: The Personages *in progress in her studio, circa 1945.*

FIGURES 14–16
This page: Installation of the Personages *in her studio in New York circa 1947.*

Opposite page, top: The Personages *stored in her studio in New York, after 1950.*

Opposite page, below: Louise Bourgeois and Personages *in 1975.*

PHOTO: ESTATE OF PETER MOORE AND VAGA, NEW YORK

forms of the sculptures, each distinctly different, evoke a group of male and female figures in close, enigmatic association. Each of the people-sized figures is an individual, but their formal distinctions are general enough to evoke endless associations, especially in terms of gender. The figures are painted in white, three of them are distinguished by blue painted hollows carved into various parts of their surfaces. The tall figure on the viewer's right is the only one lacking further distinction in terms of surface carving or added organic forms. The *Personage* in the center is surrounded by four figures, all slightly bending towards it.

Its shape evokes male and female symbols at the same time. The center figure is *Woman with Packages* (page 84) which Bourgeois has incorporated in this group piece. It carries three bags with the shape of simplified organs, painted in black and white.

With this piece, themes of forced togetherness and of isolation are reflected and given form in an even more complex way. The color (white, blue, and black) has a unifying effect and intertwines the figures. The base functions in this case as a strong conceptual element, defining the inevitability of their togetherness as a group and their need to relate and ultimately depend on each other. Ambivalent in its function, the base underscores the antagonism between individual and society, between the dynamics of a group or family on the one hand and society on the other. The title *Quarantania* adds a narrative dimension, suggesting that this group of five figures is kept at a remove from society to ensure that any disease or contagion they may have will not spread. The number of the group correspond both to Bourgeois' family in which she grew up in France as well as to the family that she and Goldwater raised in America.[13] *Quarantania* can be seen as embodying the highly personal, yet existential meanings of

FIGURE 17
Quarantania *(1947–1953). Cast bronze, white, black, and blue patina. Collection of the artist.*
PHOTO: CHRISTOPHER BURKE

separation and cultural dislocation, resulting from Bourgeois' experience as an immigrant in 1938, and from the war and its consequences. *Quarantania* also manifests, especially if seen in the context of the early 1950s, when this version of the piece was completed, a decidedly political dimension. It was the time of the Cold War and the McCarthy era with America's isolationist politics at its peak. But *Quarantania* contains, like every work of this artist, personal memories as well, reflecting Bourgeois' relationship with her families in France and in America. The coincidental appearance of her husband in the photograph seems to underline this assumption.

A different version in progress appears in a photograph from 1969 (fig. 18). Bourgeois and Robert Goldwater are both standing behind the sculpture, the artist on a ladder holding a dark fabric, while Goldwater, holding the fabric on the other side, talks to the photographer. It is the only known document showing both the artist and her husband involved with the early work. Goldwater, an art historian and critic, was among the first critics to write about *Quarantania*. His essay "What is Modern Sculpture" was published by the Museum of Modern Art in 1969, the same year as the photograph of the couple with the piece. Goldwater, in the part of his essay referring to *Quarantania*, underlined the "symbolic reference" of the piece. Based on Bourgeois' thoughts and concerns and his conversations with her, although without mentioning this, he stressed the symbolic expression of the closeness and dependence of the figures on the one hand, their silence and loneliness on the other. His description reads like the conjuration of the mutual feelings of the family he had raised with Bourgeois: "Here is a human group, its members alike but various, leaning toward one another in an intensity of feeling that unites them even as it leaves each one silent and alone."[14] Interestingly, the reproduction he is referring to shows yet another version of the same sculpture (fig. 19). Compared to the version finished in 1953 (fig. 17) and to the piece in figure 18, two short monolithic pieces had been added, leaning without fixation against the figure in the center. The base is in both reproductions from 1969 covered with cloth, adding to the impression of a work in progress. Thus in the late 1960s Bourgeois was still engaged with a sculpture more than twenty years after she had began working on it.

Goldwater, who taught at different universities and in 1957 became the first director of the Museum of Primitive Art in New York (until 1963), was the author of *Primitivism*

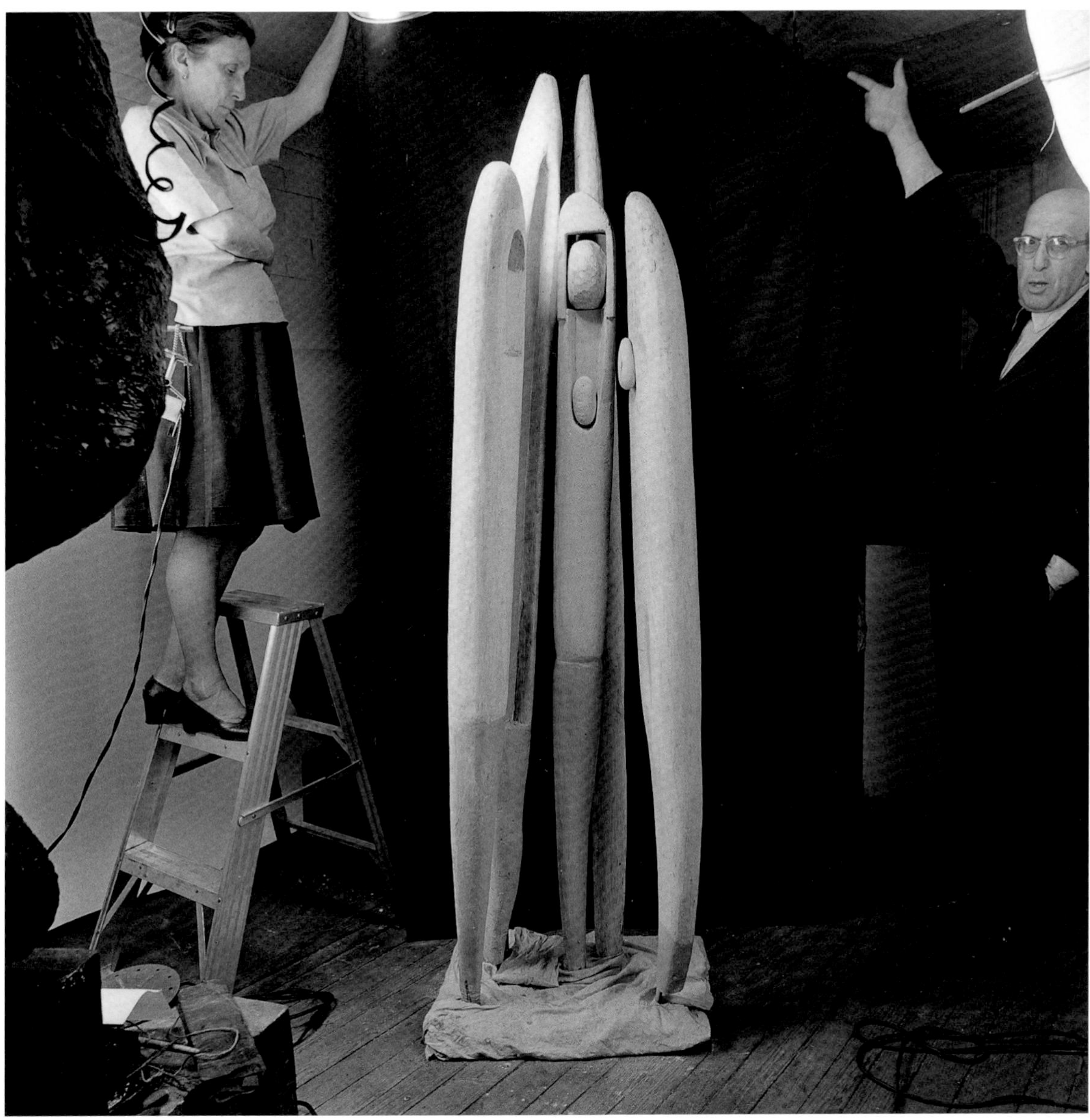

in Modern Painting, published in 1938, the year when he met and married Louise Bourgeois in Paris. His book is a groundbreaking study of the historical and aesthetic problems raised by the influence of African and Oceanic arts on modern painters. Goldwater's studies, but especially this publication, made him a specialist in the history of the development of the relationship between non-Western arts and modern artists. Goldwater was particularly interested in the reception and reactions by the artists.[15] In his writings, he addressed the relations between anthropological and aesthetic studies of non-Western arts. There is no doubt that living with an artist made him even more aware of the complex triangular relationship between the artist, the anthropologist, and the art historian.

FIGURE 18
Louise Bourgeois and Robert Goldwater in 1969 with Quarantania.

PHOTO: ESTATE OF PETER MOORE AND VAGA, NEW YORK

FIGURE 19
Quarantania, *reproduced in Goldwater's essay in 1969.*

PHOTO: ESTATE OF PETER MOORE AND VAGA, NEW YORK

Bourgeois has always refused to talk about the intellectual relationship with her husband.[16] Even if there can be no doubt about the clear distinction between the activities of Bourgeois and Goldwater as well as their point of view, they both shared a similar knowledge and interest in the tangible and symbolic aspects of objects—their use, how and why they were conceived, and how they were circulated among individuals and within a community. And their different point of views must have resulted in a very interesting combination of knowledge and experience about the use and meanings of cult objects, artifacts, and art.

The fact that Bourgeois continued to work on *Quarantania* even after the first version of the piece was finished in 1953 reflects an almost narcissistic dialogue with her own work. The artist has described this process of revision and reconfiguration of existing works as "cannibalistic."[17] Throughout her career she repeatedly returns to certain pieces that develop themes that have a particular urgency in the work. *Quarantania* is one of the most complex pieces of the early work. It seizes the whole range of the deeply problematic and painful relationship between individual and society, a field of tension that for Bourgeois holds a political as well as a profoundly personal dimension.

REAL SPACE AND ABSTRACT SPACE

From the beginning, emotional necessity rather than an interest in any artistic vocabulary per se seems to have dictated the making of the *Personages*. Several decades after she worked on the sculptures, Bourgeois stated: "The figures on the roof had nothing to do with sculpture, they meant physical presences. That was an attempt not only recreating the past but controlling it."[18] In the same interview, Bourgeois further explained the strong motivations to create the *Personages* and their very personal function to reconstruct rather than represent reality. By comparing the real space of the roof and the stairs in her house on 18th Street with the space in a gallery, Bourgeois emphasized the distinction between the two settings: "The dynamism of the presence in a claustrophobic space such as the top of the stairs under the roof was much more dynamic than the gallery.... But the gallery would not have permitted me to place my *Personages* in a closet which in effect is the way they were conceived."[19]

Nevertheless, the installation in three shows at the Peridot Gallery in 1949, 1950, and

1953 became an important part in the process of testing the sculptures in different environments. The psychological tension between intimacy and isolation, between silence and dialogue became the starting point for the installation. The tensions between the sculptures were expressed through the symbolism of their geometric relationship in space. In a comment on her text "The Puritan" from 1947 Bourgeois mentioned Euclidean geometry as a means to express complex emotional relationships.[20] Geometry as a rational means seems a methodological equivalent to tame emotions, to perceive, measure and control feelings—an obvious parallel to the tradition of American pragmatism.[21] In 1976, Bourgeois explained for the first time how she had conceived of the installation at Peridot: her concept had been to translate the psychological drama into the visual organization of the space: "I mean solid geometry as a symbol for emotional security.... It comes naturally to me to express emotions through relations between geometrical elements, in two dimensions or three dimensions. In the Peridot exhibition the disposition of and relations between the figures, grouped in twos and threes or isolated, represents a readable floor graph."[22] In the gallery setting, the "space of the viewer" became the "space of the maker."[23] By referring to the environmental sculpture of the 1960s and 1970s, Bourgeois emphasized her need in the 1940s to use real objects in real space.[24] Showing them in public allowed the artist to move on to new conceptual questions in her work: "There is such a shock after a show. A show is an experience and after a show an artist is a different person. He moves on—so does the work. So the space that was so indispensable when I needed a real space with real six-foot people, that need disappeared completely. It was resolved and forgotten. I could move in abstract space."[25] But the intense exploration of the physical space of her private environment and the experience of the installation in the gallery were inevitable for the transition from real to abstract space.

ANIMISM VERSUS MODERNIST LOGIC

Unlike the surrealists who analyzed, transformed, and exploited the psychological dimensions and irrational potential of everyday objects, Bourgeois tended to make sculptures her domestic objects, using them as tools with which she confronted and redefined her inner world. By placing them in different contexts, Bourgeois tested and investigated their status and their inherent qualities as sculpture, their ability to interact with different forms of architecture, with nature, and with people. As shown above, she was especially interested in environments lacking the physical and ideological marks of professional art places. By leaving the protected, but also predetermined and historically charged context of the gallery or the museum, where art was automatically declared and perceived as art, Bourgeois investigated the role and status of sculpture itself. The *process* of making the sculptures, reworking them and exposing them to different, mostly private milieus, was more important than showing them in public. Investigating the *Personages* over several years in different contexts also allowed Bourgeois to keep control over her sculptures, to lengthen the time she could activate them on her own before they would eventually be separated from her as the maker.

One of the most striking features of the early work, the sculpture as well as the drawings, the prints and, although to a lesser degree, the paintings, is their austerity. The rawness of the forms as well as of the technical execution, an almost artless simplicity seems to be their common denominator. This is especially true with the *Personages*, whose intentionally unsophisticated forms predispose them for an everyday, practical use, removing them from their function as artworks. Most of them have, similar to primitive utilitarian objects, little or no surface decoration, their materials are unpolished, the wood patina is as simple as that of everyday objects. The use of colors underscores the austerity of the sculptures and their lack of any "romanticism of materials." [26] The object seems to be nothing more than the visual and practical embodiment of its function. Instead of traditional aesthetic values like technical innovation, refinement, complexity, or even virtuosity, we find simplicity, imperfection, austerity, and rawness. The crude unpolished appearance of the wood sculptures and of Bourgeois' early work in general is opposed to the principles of a society in which everything is based on the pragmatism and streamlined cleanliness of mass production and on the socio-politically motivated ideology of optimism. Seen as a group, the *Personages* evoke the nostalgic world of used, worn-out objects, the melancholy of age.

But there are additional characteristics that indicate the world out of which they were created. The *Portrait of Jean-Louis* (page 78) was the only piece among the *Personages* whose final display depended on a wall as support. An installation view from the first exhibition at the Peridot Gallery, with the same figure standing on the floor like the other *Personages* (fig. 20), proves that *Portrait of Jean-Louis* went through a process of exploring several ways of presentation as well, changing the very meaning of the sculpture. *Portrait of Jean-Louis* reveals, through the violent combination of two different spheres, the human body and the skyscraper, a tendency towards drastic concision. The lower part with pelvis and legs turns, without transition, in the upper part into a repetitive high-rise structure.[27] Interestingly, Bourgeois used the metaphor of the skyscraper in another portrait of a child. *Dagger Child*, installed in the Peridot show not far from *Portrait of Jean-Louis* next to *The Blind Leading the Blind* (fig. 20), is based on the shape of the Chrysler Building, one of the most famous Manhattan skyscrapers completed in 1930.[28] By combining two different realities, the portrait of a child and the representation of high-rise architecture, Bourgeois created powerful expressions of self-assertion. Both *Portrait of Jean-Louis* and *Dagger Child* generate an atmosphere of dialogue and defense which stems from the inherent antagonism of the iconography, the firm frontality and verticality as much as from the crude execution of the pieces.[29]

The violent fusion of form and content is one of Bourgeois' essential conceptual principles. The mostly monolithic *Personages* from the 1940s as well as the assembled *Personages* from the early 1950s manifest both a fundamental, intentionally unresolved contradiction between rigorous form and an utter lack of interest in the aesthetics of form. The emotional power of the object, its animistic component, is more important to Bourgeois than form as an aesthetic issue. Form comes into being when overwhelming feelings erupt.[30]

FIGURE 20
Peridot Gallery, New York, "Louise Bourgeois, Recent Work 1947–1949: Seventeen Standing Figures in Wood," October 3–29, 1949.
PHOTO: JEREMIAH RUSSELL

Like reductionism or the fusion of opposites, repetition as a formal and conceptual principle reflects Bourgeois' methodical logic as well. Repetition breaks the representational function of materials and forms aesthetically as well as conceptually. In the maker's

perspective, "repetition gives a physical reality to experience."[31] Obsessive repetition leads to emphasis on quantification, which then becomes in Bourgeois' vocabulary, like the symbol of the skyscraper, a powerful form of intensification. Repetition, as the artist has stated over and over again, is the equivalent of emotional urgency. Repetition as a methodical means is especially true with the group of the segmented *Personages* created in the early 1950s, which are constructed by pieces of wood stacked vertically or strung together along a metal spine (fig. 22). Here, execution becomes a highly ritualized act of adding, stacking, pinning pieces—a ritual of repetition.[32] And as such, the ritual reflects both systematic logic as well as the unpredictable and irrational sides of obsession and compulsion. Thus, repetition emphasizes both the rational and the emotional component of Bourgeois' method.

FIGURES 21–22
Opposite page: Peridot Gallery, New York, 1950. From left: Breasted Woman, Winged Figure, *and* Pillar.

PHOTO: AARON SISKIND

Above: Louise Bourgeois in the mid-1960s with Femme Volage, *1951.*

Some of the *Personages* (*Paddle Woman, Spoon Woman, Needle Woman*) have almost archetypical titles. But as the titles suggest, the sculptures are nameless, seemingly part of a deeply personal world. And indeed, the crude, elementary, in some cases amorphous quality, the coarseness of materials and forms, indicate savagery, non-integration. Physically raw and emotionally charged, the figures become alive to a degree that they seem "to bleed."[33] *Pregnant Woman* seems especially indicative in this context of the emotionally charged figure in modern society. As seen above (fig. 12), *Pregnant Woman* in an earlier version was a clothed figure. The shape and meaning of the piece oscillates between a raw piece of wood, a primitive, worn-out tool, and the simplified biomorphic shape of what the title suggests, a pregnant body. By wrapping the figure in her own cloth, Bourgeois strengthened the tangible concreteness of the emotions that were at the origin of the figure. At the same time, the cloth makes the absence of a living body more irritating. The solidity of the figure in wood is overlaid with the seemingly corresponding, but actually contradictory layer of the cloth, pushing the representational nature of the sculpture over the edge.[34]

The precarious execution and the fragility of the *Personages* is in itself a powerful rejection of the patriarchal idea of monumentality. Rawness, reductionism, fusion of opposites, repetition—as methodical and stylistic principles all contribute to the expression of emotional intensity which is the motor of Bourgeois' art. The multilayered symbolism enhances the emotional charge. With the *Personages*, the horizon of associations ranges from archeological objects, tribal fetishes, objects of warfare (dagger), and everyday utilitarian objects (knife, paddle, needle) to symbols of modern, highly organized urban structures (skyscrapers). In its primal state as magical cult object, the function of sculpture was a means to ensure its maker's survival.[35] Bourgeois' sculptures echo the primeval origins of artworks, while they also indicate a highly personal, hermetic iconography. The significance and power of the *Personages* lays exactly in the combination of animism and the formalist idiosyncrasies of twentieth century modern art.

The *Personages* are the first powerful body of work of an artist whose idiosyncratic and highly innovative work has brought a unique vision to American art. More than that, Bourgeois' early sculpture offers a contribution to a new perception and role of the artwork as an object. Her early sculptures crystallize emotional and cultural meanings in an unprecedented fashion. For many decades, Bourgeois has developed and maintained her own distinctive vocabulary. Even after becoming a central figure of the art world, she remains invisible in public. Profoundly apart from the present-day art world in which her work is shown and celebrated, Bourgeois insists on exploiting the mechanisms of her own productivity and excavating the territories of her psyche. But what she offers the viewers transcends her own private story, and the common reality of present-day art.

Many thanks go to Jerry Gorovoy for his advice and help in shedding light on the history of the making of the Personages *and to Wendy Williams for generously sharing the material in the Louise Bourgeois archives. I thank Sarah Eckhardt for her excellent research assistance with this essay. I am very grateful to Karen Hewitt for her critical reading and substantial help in editing this article.* JH

NOTES

1. The first three sculptures cast in bronze were *Sleeping Figure*, *Listening One*, and *Spring*. I thank Jerry Gorovoy for sharing this information with me.

2. Wye. 1982, 16.

3. Louise Bourgeois from "Freud's Toys," *Artforum*, January 1990, 111–113. All quotes in this section are from this essay.

4. Bourgeois. 1998, 51.

5. Susi Bloch. "An Interview with Louise Bourgeois," *The Art Journal*, vol. 35, no. 4, Summer 1976, 373.

6. "In that period these materials came from the makers of water towers for high buildings in New York. The water towers which sit on the top of the buildings were made of a special wood, were made of redwood of California." Alain Kirili. "The Passion for Sculpture: A Conversation with Louise Bourgeois," *Arts Magazine*, March 1989, 72.

7. Gorovoy/Tilkin. 1999, 38.

8. Bourgeois in 1954, her first published statement on the *Personages*. See page 34 in this volume. Strick. 1994, 8.

9. One of the most striking examples for Bourgeois' equation between a human body and an object of daily use is her sarcastic description of the role of Sadie, a young English woman, who was hired by her father in 1972 to serve as governess to Louise Bourgeois and her siblings, as "a standard piece of furniture." Gorovoy/Tilkin. 1999, 16.

10. Kirili. 1989, 72.

11. Bourgeois in Philip Pearlstein, "The Private Myth," *Artnews*, vol. 60, Sept. 1961, 45.

12. Lippard mentions the "portable brother." Lippard. 1976, 240.

13. Bourgeois talks about the symbolism of the number five and the pentagon as a reflection of her family situation in Kuspit. 1988, 68f.

14. Goldwater. 1969, 97. This is not the first time Goldwater had written about Bourgeois' work. See Robert Goldwater "La sculpture actuelle a New York," *Cimaise*, vol. 4, November/December 1956, 24–28. In this essay, published in French, Goldwater positioned Bourgeois in the movement of recent American sculpture.

15. Goldwater described himself as "having some sympathy for the point of view of the artist, an attitude not always shared by my colleagues who come from other disciplines." Robert Goldwater. *A Memorial Exhibition: 1973*, The Museum of Primitive Art, New York, 1973, 18.

16. In the interview with Donald Kuspit, Bourgeois mentioned symbolism as an interest she shared with her husband. Kuspit. 1988, 52.

17. "I have a cannibalistic attitude to my work. I would let it sit until I could use it to make new work. It had to reach a certain state of familiarity. Then I could incorporate it in a new work." Bourgeois in Kuspit. 1988, 73.

18. Bloch. 1976, 373.

19. Ibid.

20. Bourgeois. 1998. 55.

21. In the tradition of American pragmatism and empiricism, it is assumed that emotional and mental phenomena can only be understood with rational methods, that is to say, with experimental studies of the physical, organic human being.

22. Bloch. 1976, 372.

23. Ibid.

24. "That is to say the necessity for the artist to function in a real space is carried on during the show." Ibid.

25. Ibid., 373.

26. Bourgeois in the late 1960s, see Strick. 1994, 8.

27. Helfenstein in Gorovoy/Tilkin. 1999, 21.

28. Ibid.

29. In a statement in the 1990s, Bourgeois referred to human experience of distance, lack of communication, and introspection, when she, adding another dimension to the metaphor of the skyscraper, noted: "My skyscrapers are not really about New York. Skyscrapers reflect a human condition. They do not touch." Meyer-Thoss. 1992, 178.

30. See Helfenstein in Gorovoy/Tilkin. 1999, 22.

31. Meyer-Thoss. 1992, 194.

32. As has been recognized previously, geometric pieces like *Mortise* (page 91) or *Memling Dawn* (page 92) call to mind minimal sculptures by Carl Andre done over a decade later. See Strick. 1994, 28.

33. Maurice Merlau-Ponty. *The Prose of the World*, Evanston: Northwestern University Press, 1973, 152.

34. After 1996, sculptures and figures made of cloth and dresses begin to appear frequently in Bourgeois' work.

35. Josef Helfenstein, "The Power of Intimacy," *Parkett*, no. 27, 1991, 33ff.

artist's statement

An artist's words are always to be taken cautiously. The finished work is often a stranger to, and sometimes very much at odds with what the artist felt, or wished to express when he began. At best the artist does what he can rather than what he wants to do. After the battle is over and the damage faced up to, the result may be surprisingly dull—but sometimes it is surprisingly interesting. The mountain brought forth a mouse, but the bee will create a miracle of beauty and order. Asked to enlighten us on their creative process, both would be embarrassed, and probably uninterested. The artist who discusses the so-called meaning of his work is usually describing a literary side-issue. The core of his original impulse is to be found, if at all, in the work itself.

Just the same, the artist must say what he feels:

My work grows from the duel between the isolated individual and the shared awareness of the group. At first I made single figures without any freedom at all: blind houses without any openings, any relation to the outside world. Later, tiny windows started to appear. And then I began to develop an interest in the relationship between two figures. The figures of this phase are turned in on themselves, but they try to be together even though they may not succeed in reaching each other.

Gradually the relations between the figures I made became freer and more subtle, and now I see my works as groups of objects relating to each other. Although ultimately each can and does stand alone, the figures can be grouped in various ways and fashions, and each time the tension of their relations makes for a different formal arrangement. For this reason the figures are placed in the ground the way people would place themselves in the street to talk to each other. And this is why they grow from a single point—a minimum base of immobility which suggests an always possible change.

In my most recent work these relations become clearer and more intimate. Now the single work has its own complex of parts, each of which is similar, yet different from the others. But there is still the feeling with which I began—the drama of one among many.

The look of my figures is abstract, and to the spectator they may not appear to be figures at all. They are the expression, in abstract terms, of emotions and states of awareness. Eighteenth-century painters made "conversation pieces"; my sculptures might be called "confrontation pieces."

Louise Bourgeois, 1954

This statement by Louise Bourgeois was first published in 1954 by the Walker Art Center, Minneapolis, in *Design Quarterly*, no. 30, 18.

PAINTINGS

REPARATION
Oil on linen,
1938–40
no. 1

UNTITLED
Oil on canvas,
1945
no. 2

UNTITLED
Oil on canvas,
1946
no. 3

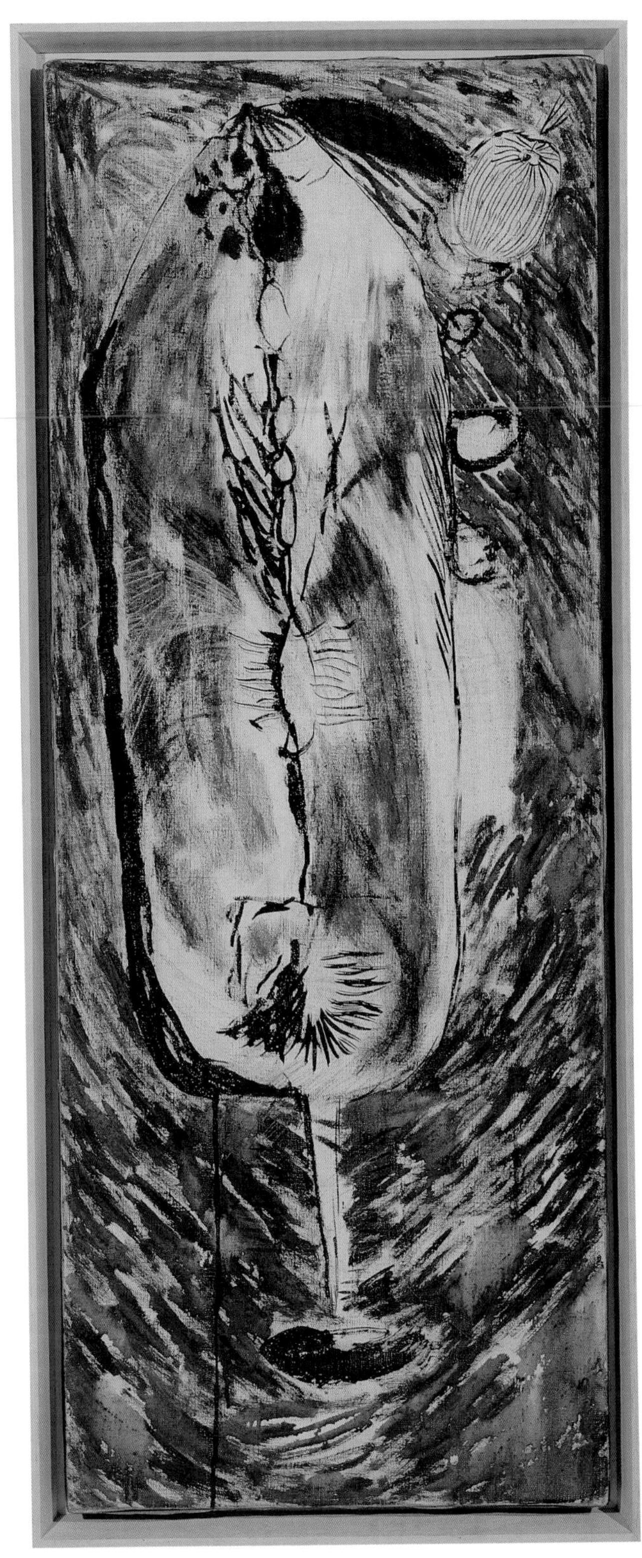

ONE WAY TRAFFIC
Oil on canvas, 1946
no. 4

UNTITLED
Oil and chalk on canvas, 1946
no. 5

UNTITLED
Oil, charcoal and pastel on canvas, 1946

no. 6

UNTITLED
Oil on linen,
1946–47
no. 7

UNTITLED
Oil on wood,
1946–47
no. 9

IT IS SIX FIFTEEN
Oil on canvas,
1946–48
no. 10

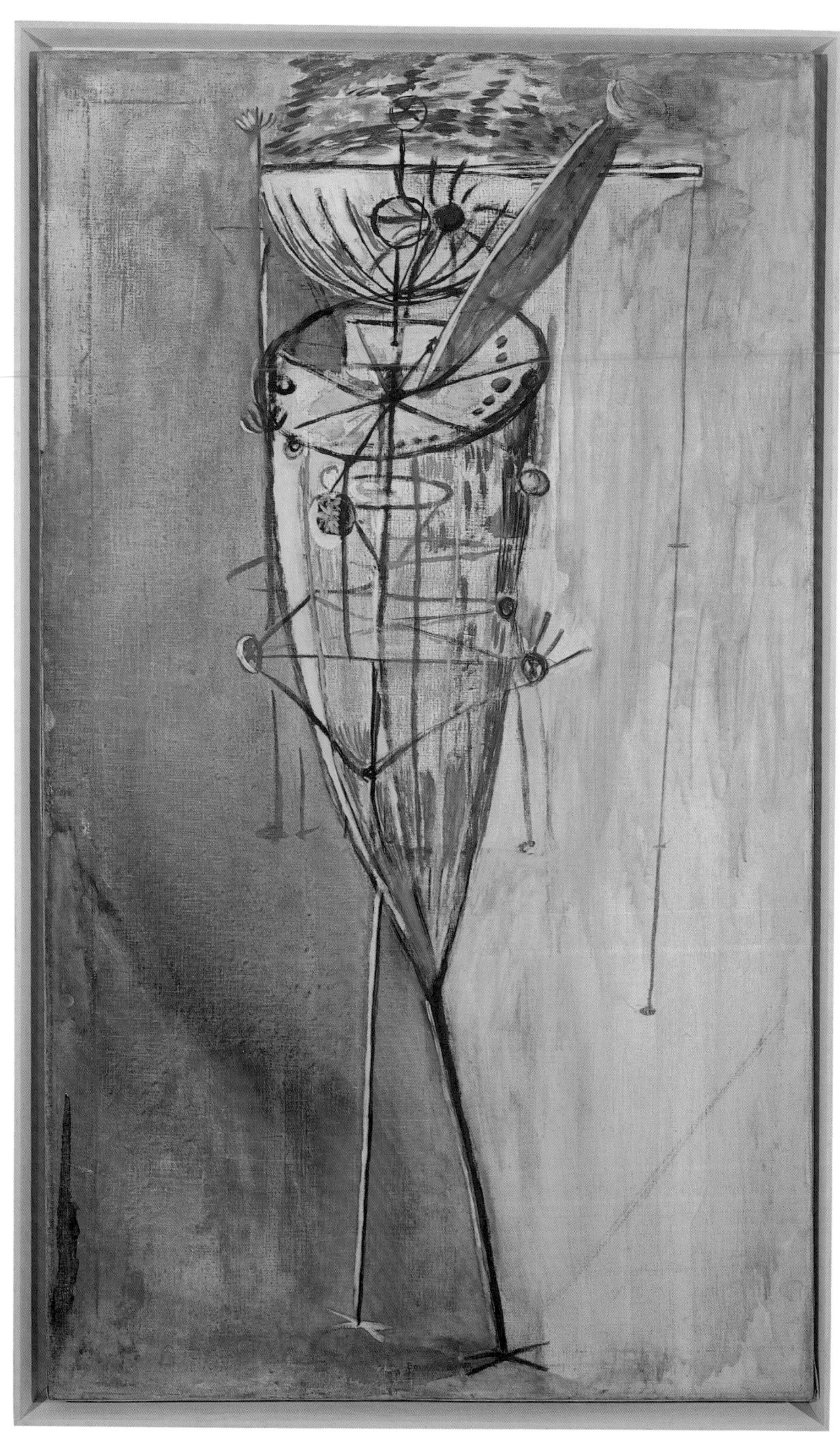

UNTITLED
Oil on canvas,
1947
no. 12

REGRETTABLE INCIDENT IN THE LOUVRE PALACE
Oil on canvas, 1947
no. 11

UNTITLED
Oil on canvas,
1946–47
no. 8

UNTITLED
Oil on canvas,
1948
no. 13

WOMAN IN PROCESS OF PLACING A BEAM IN HER BAG
Oil on canvas, 1948
no. 14

NO SWEARING ALLOWED
Oil on canvas, 1949
no. 15

PRINTS

HE DISAPPEARED INTO COMPLETE SILENCE
Suite of 9 engravings with text, 1947
no. 16

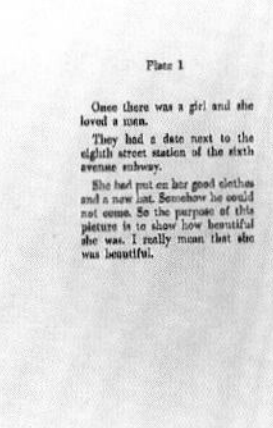

Plate 1

Once there was a girl and she loved a man.

They had a date next to the eighth street station of the sixth avenue subway.

She had put on her good clothes and a new hat. Somehow he could not come. So the purpose of this picture is to show how beautiful she was. I really mean that she was beautiful.

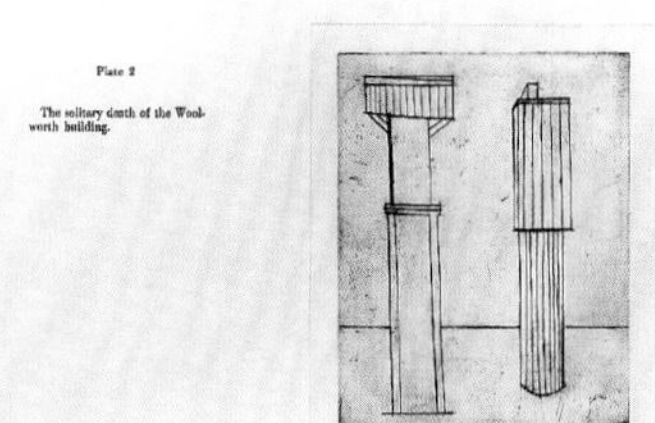

Plate 2

The solitary death of the Woolworth building.

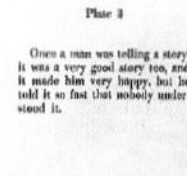

Plate 3

Once a man was telling a story, it was a very good story too, and it made him very happy, but he told it so fast that nobody understood it.

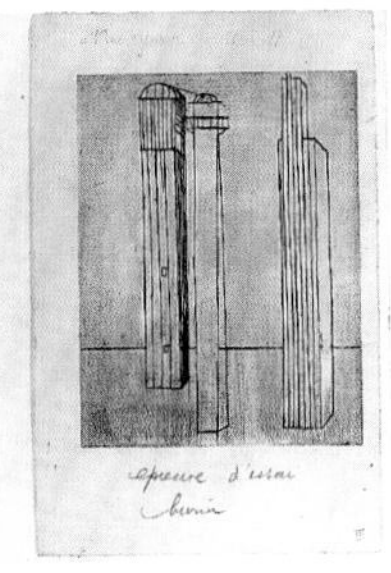

Plate 4

In the mountains of Central France forty years ago, sugar was a rare product.

Children got one piece of it at Christmas time.

A little girl that I knew when she was my mother used to be very fond and very jealous of it.

She made a hole in the ground and hid her sugar in, and she always forgot that the earth is damp.

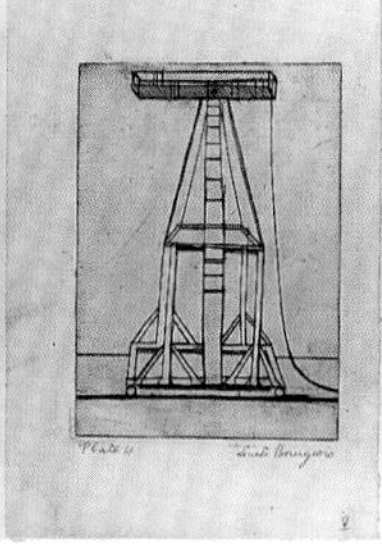

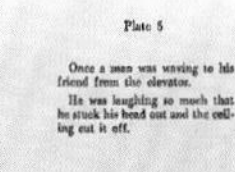

Plate 5

Once a man was waving to his friend from the elevator.

He was laughing so much that he stuck his head out and the ceiling cut it off.

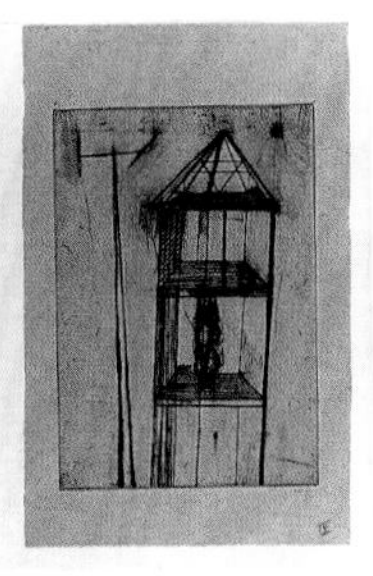

Plate 6

Leprosarium, Louisiana.

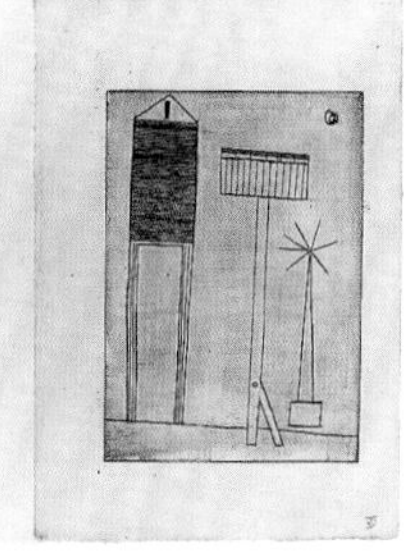

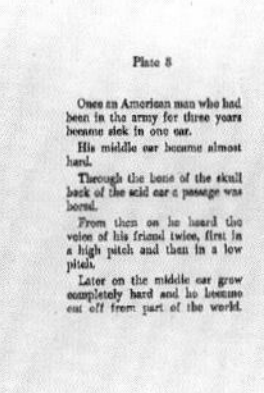

Plate 7

Once a man was angry at his wife, he cut her in small pieces, made a stew of her.

Then he telephoned to his friends and asked them for a cocktail-and-stew party.

Then all came and had a good time.

Plate 8

Once an American man who had been in the army for three years became sick in one ear.

His middle ear became almost hard.

Through the bone of the skull back of the said ear a passage was bored.

From then on he heard the voice of his friend twice, first in a high pitch and then in a low pitch.

Later on the middle ear grew completely hard and he became cut off from part of the world.

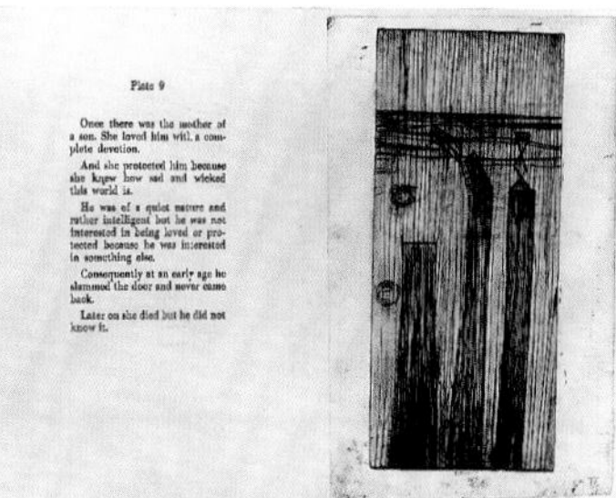

Plate 9

Once there was the mother of a son. She loved him with a complete devotion.

And she protected him because she knew how sad and wicked this world is.

He was of a quiet nature and rather intelligent but he was not interested in being loved or protected because he was interested in something else.

Consequently at an early age he slammed the door and never came back.

Later on she died but he did not know it.

Plate 1

Once there was a girl and she loved a man.

They had a date next to the eighth street station of the sixth avenue subway.

She had put on her good clothes and a new hat. Somehow he could not come. So the purpose of this picture is to show how beautiful she was. I really mean that she was beautiful.

Plate 1
Bourgeois
I

Plate 2

The solitary death of the Woolworth building.

Plate 3

Once a man was telling a story, it was a very good story too, and it made him very happy, but he told it so fast that nobody understood it.

epreuve d'essai
burin
III

Plate 4

In the mountains of Central France forty years ago, sugar was a rare product.

Children got one piece of it at Christmas time.

A little girl that I knew when she was my mother used to be very fond and very jealous of it.

She made a hole in the ground and hid her sugar in, and she always forgot that the earth is damp.

Plate 4
Louise Bourgeois
V

Plate 5

Once a man was waving to his friend from the elevator.

He was laughing so much that he stuck his head out and the ceiling cut it off.

Plate 6

Leprosarium, Louisiana.

Plate 7

Once a man was angry at his wife, he cut her in small pieces, made a stew of her.

Then he telephoned to his friends and asked them for a cocktail-and-stew party.

Then all came and had a good time.

Plate 8

Once an American man who had been in the army for three years became sick in one ear.

His middle ear became almost hard.

Through the bone of the skull back of the said ear a passage was bored.

From then on he heard the voice of his friend twice, first in a high pitch and then in a low pitch.

Later on the middle ear grew completely hard and he became cut off from part of the world.

VIII

Plate 9

Once there was the mother of a son. She loved him with a complete devotion.

And she protected him because she knew how sad and wicked this world is.

He was of a quiet nature and rather intelligent but he was not interested in being loved or protected because he was interested in something else.

Consequently at an early age he slammed the door and never came back.

Later on she died but he did not know it.

IX

SCULPTURES

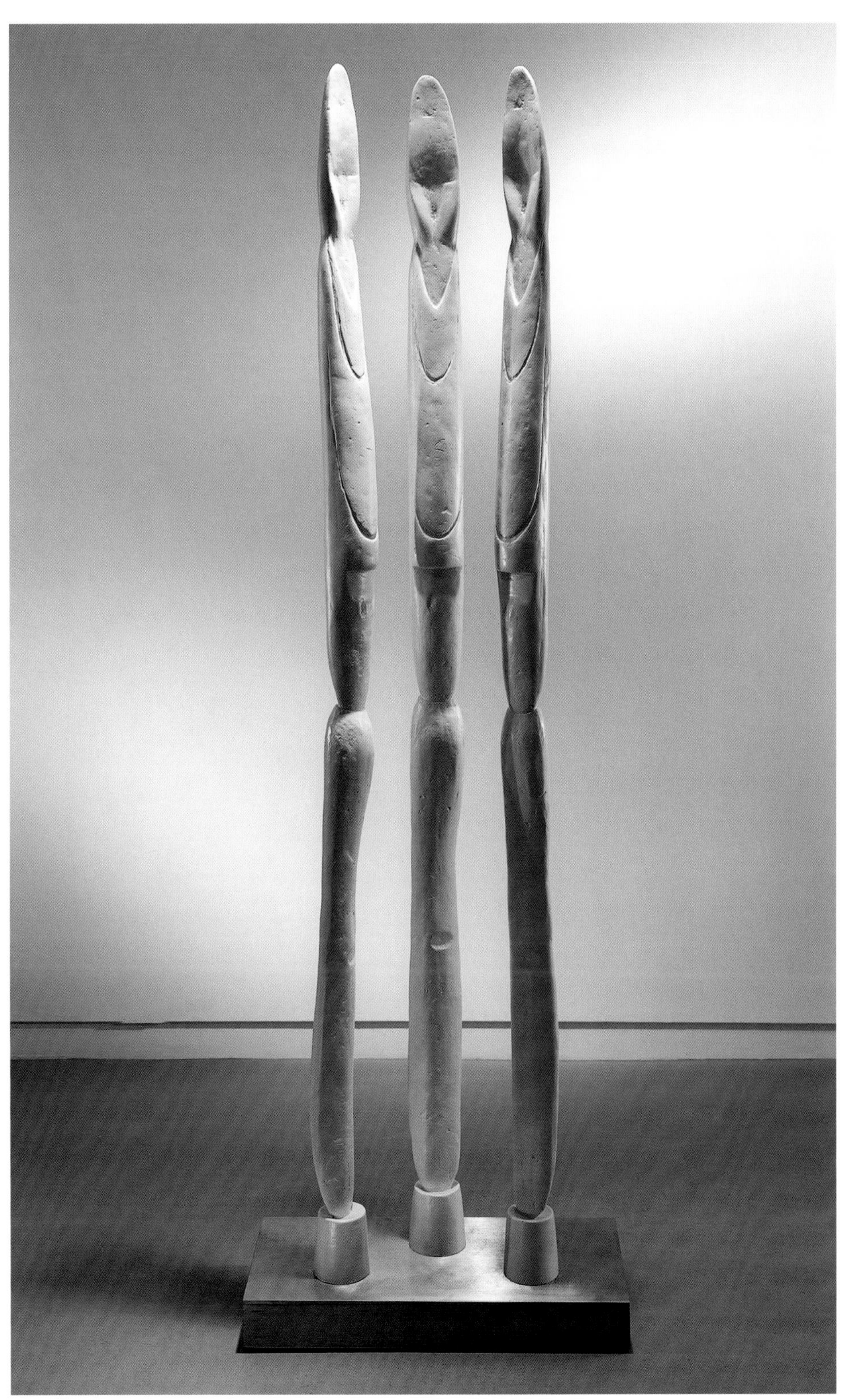

THE THREE GRACES
Bronze, painted white, 1947
no. 18

LISTENING ONE
Bronze, painted
white, 1947
no. 19

PADDLE WOMAN
Bronze, 1947
no. 20

DAGGER CHILD
Bronze, 1947–49
no. 21

NEEDLE WOMAN
Bronze, painted white, 1947–49
no. 22

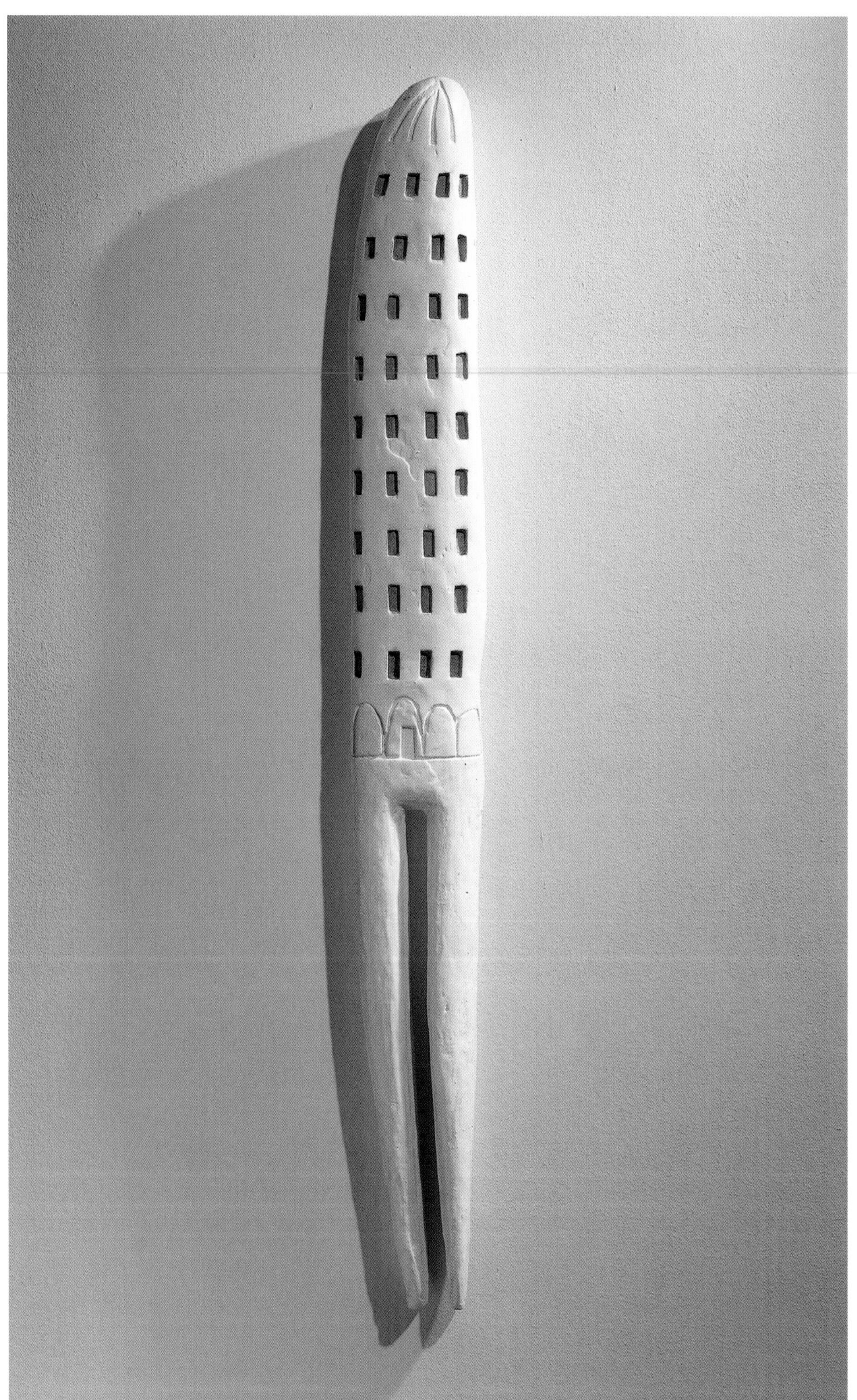

PORTRAIT OF JEAN-LOUIS
Bronze, painted white and blue, 1947–49
no. 23

BLACK FLAMES
Bronze, 1947–49
no. 24

CORNER PIECE
Bronze and paint,
1947–49
no. 26

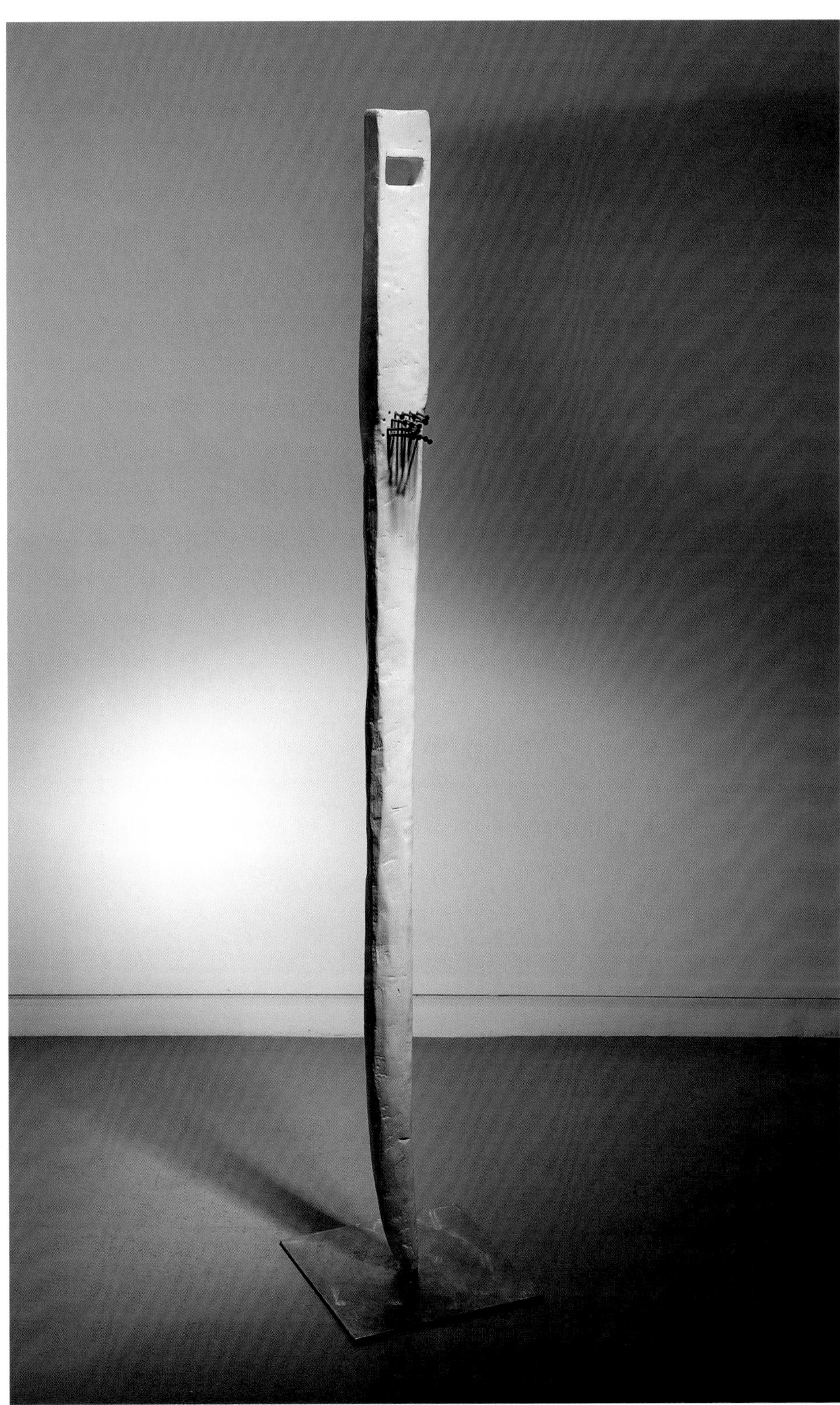

PORTRAIT OF C.Y.
Bronze, painted white, and nails, 1947–49
no. 25

PREGNANT WOMAN I
Bronze, 1947–49
no. 28

THE WINGED FIGURE
Bronze and paint, 1948
no. 29

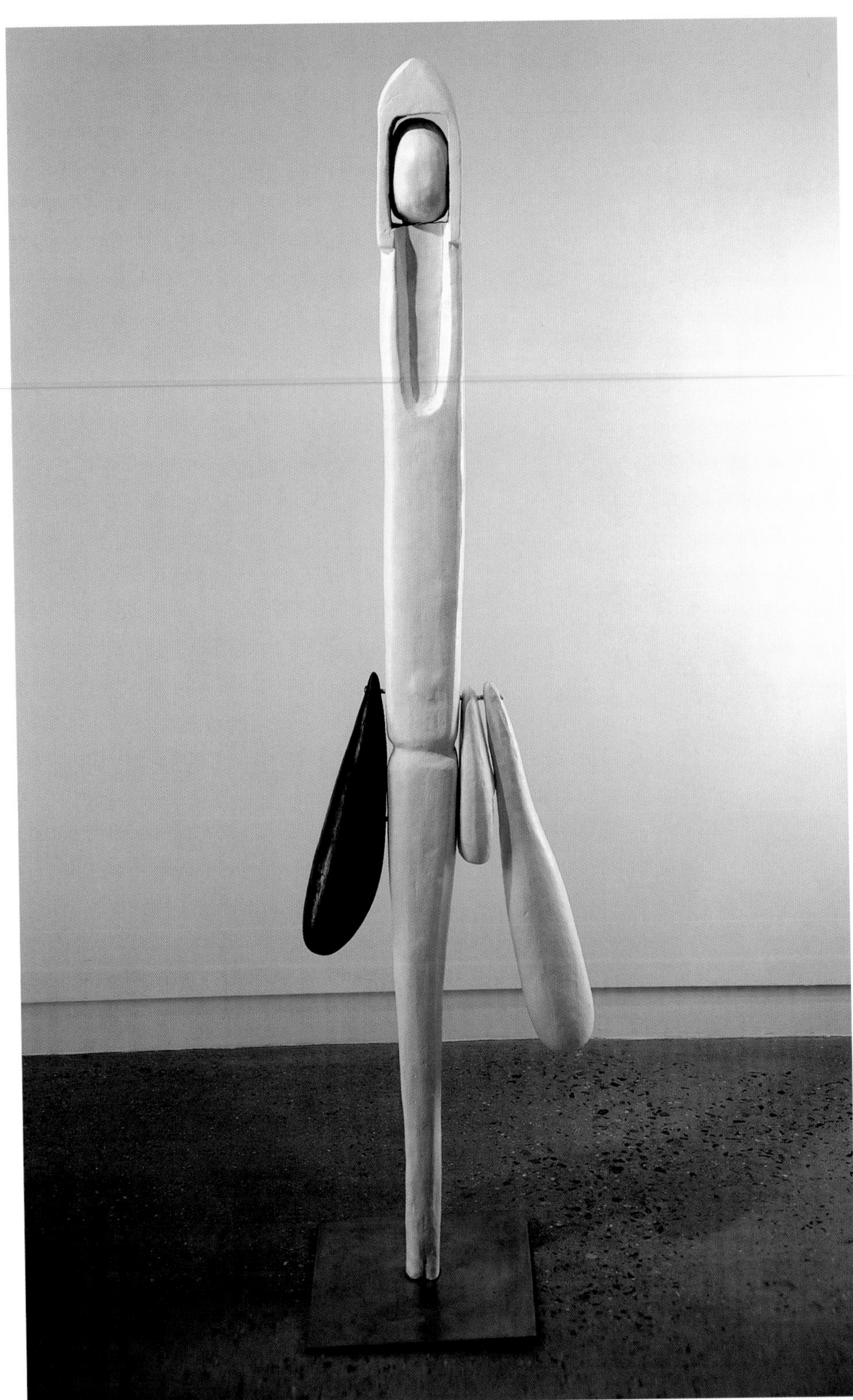

WOMAN WITH PACKAGES
Bronze, painted white and black, 1949
no. 30

QUARANTANIA
Bronze, dark patina, 1947–53
no. 38

KNIFE COUPLE
Bronze, 1949
no. 31

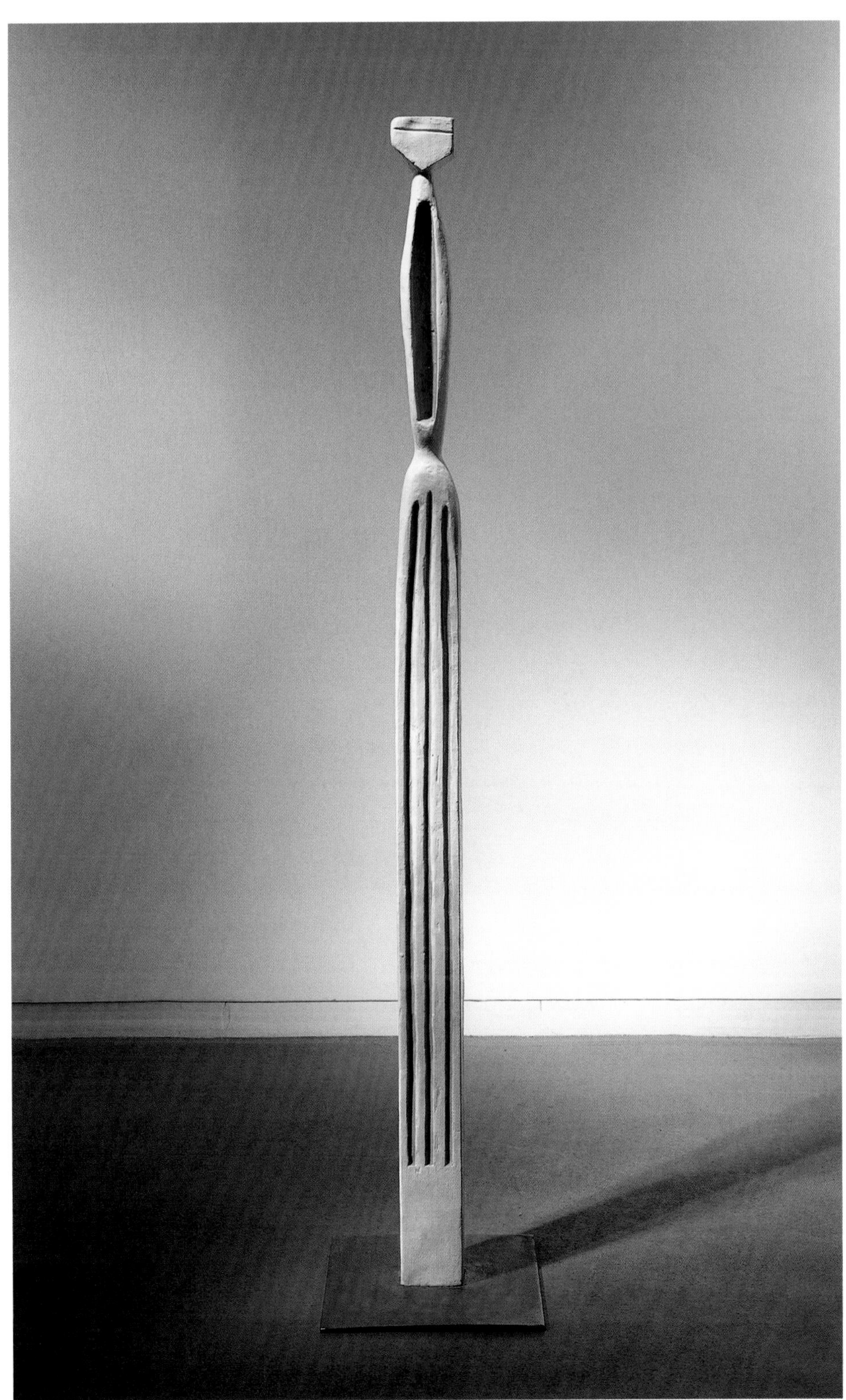

PILLAR
Bronze, painted white and blue, 1949–50
no. 32

DEPRESSION WOMAN
Bronze, painted white, 1949–50
no. 33

FRIENDLY EVIDENCE
Bronze, 1947–49
no. 34

UNTITLED
Bronze, stainless steel, and mirror, 1950
no. 35

MORTISE
Bronze, painted red and black, 1950
no. 36

MEMLING DAWN
Bronze, 1951
no. 37

THE BLIND LEADING THE BLIND
Bronze, dark patina, 1947–49
no. 27

UNTITLED
Bronze, 1953
no. 39

UNTITLED
Painted wood,
1954
no. 40

UNTITLED
Painted wood and latex, 1954–62
no. 42

ONE AND OTHERS
Painted and stained wood, 1955
no. 41

DRAWINGS

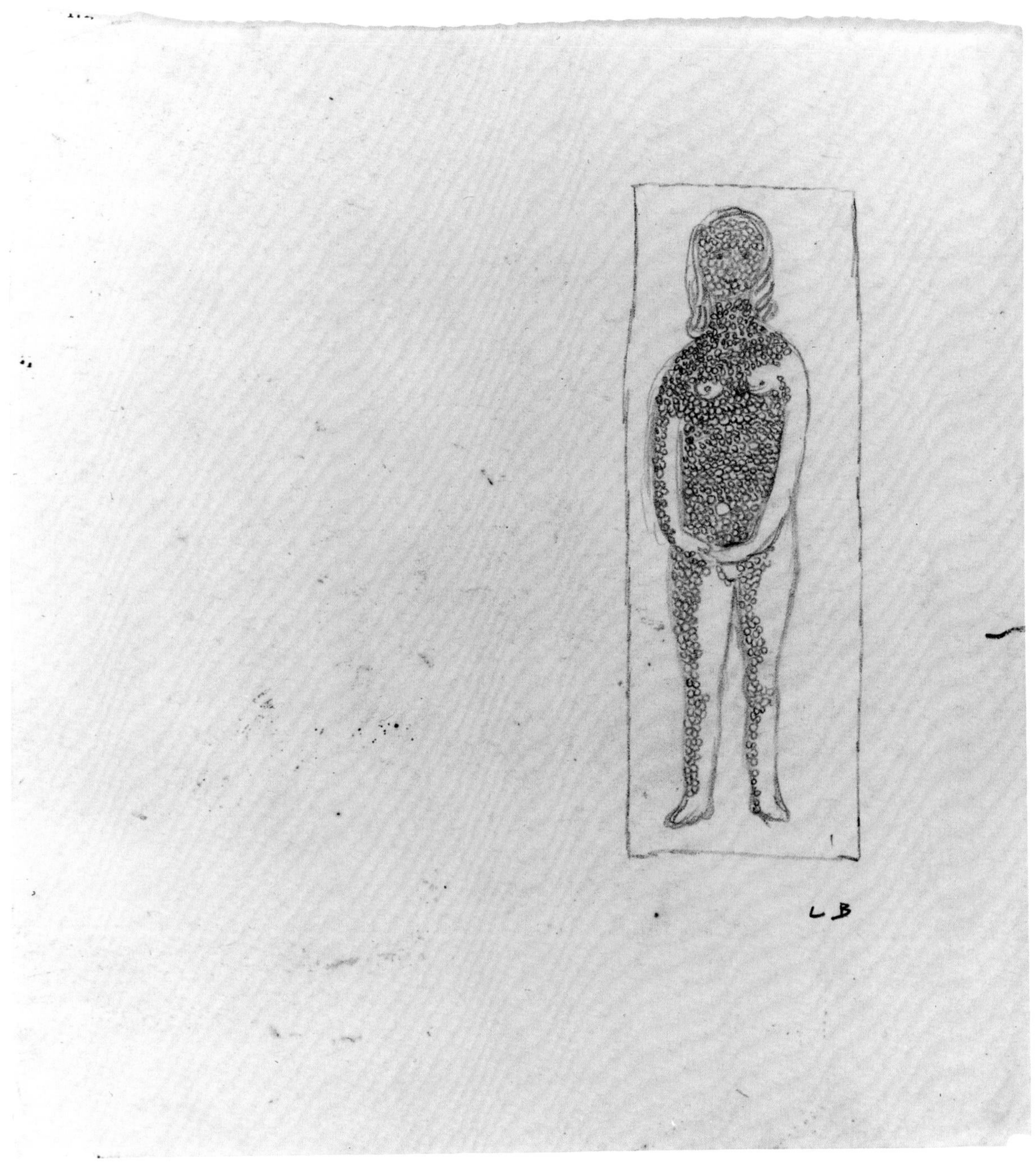

UNTITLED
Pencil on paper,
1942
no. 43

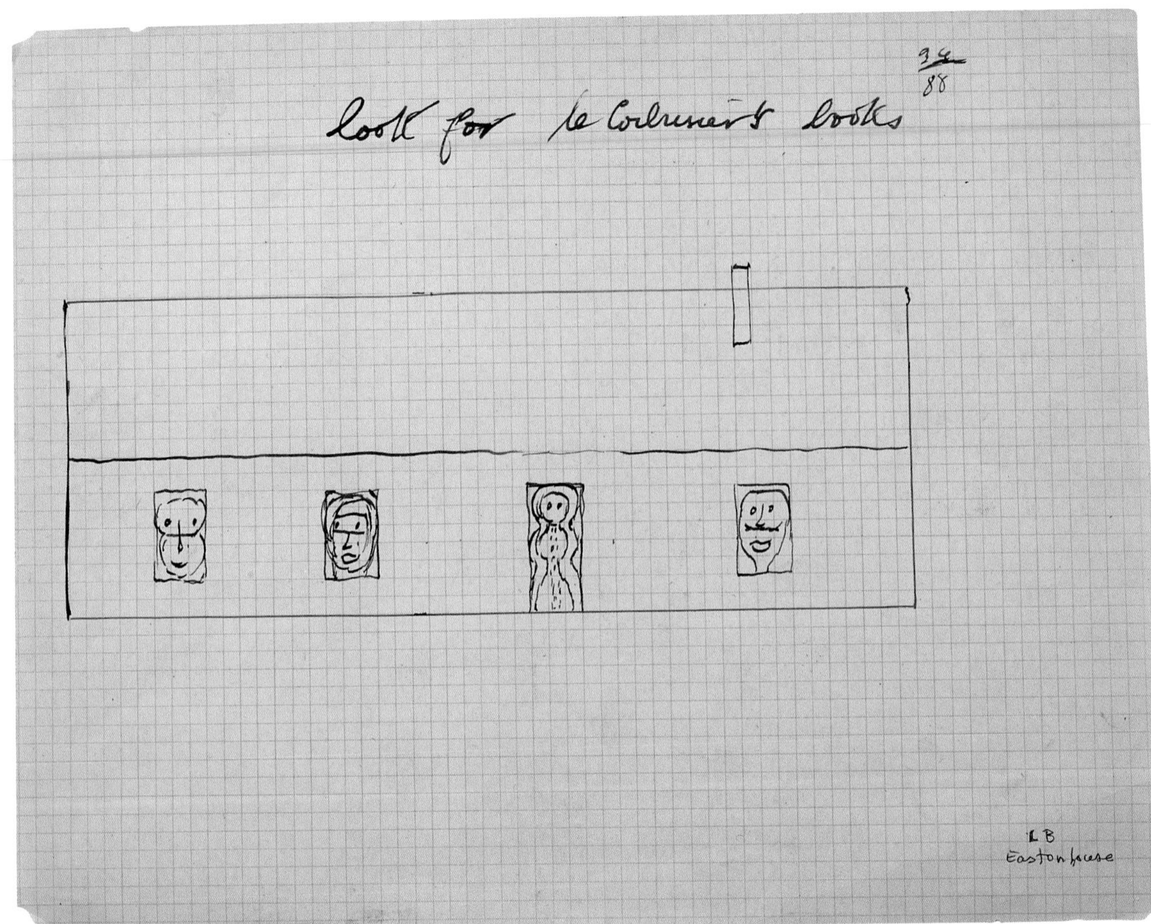

EASTON HOUSE

Ink on graph paper, 1946

no. 44

UNTITLED (DOUBLE SIDED)
Pencil on paper, 1946
no. 45

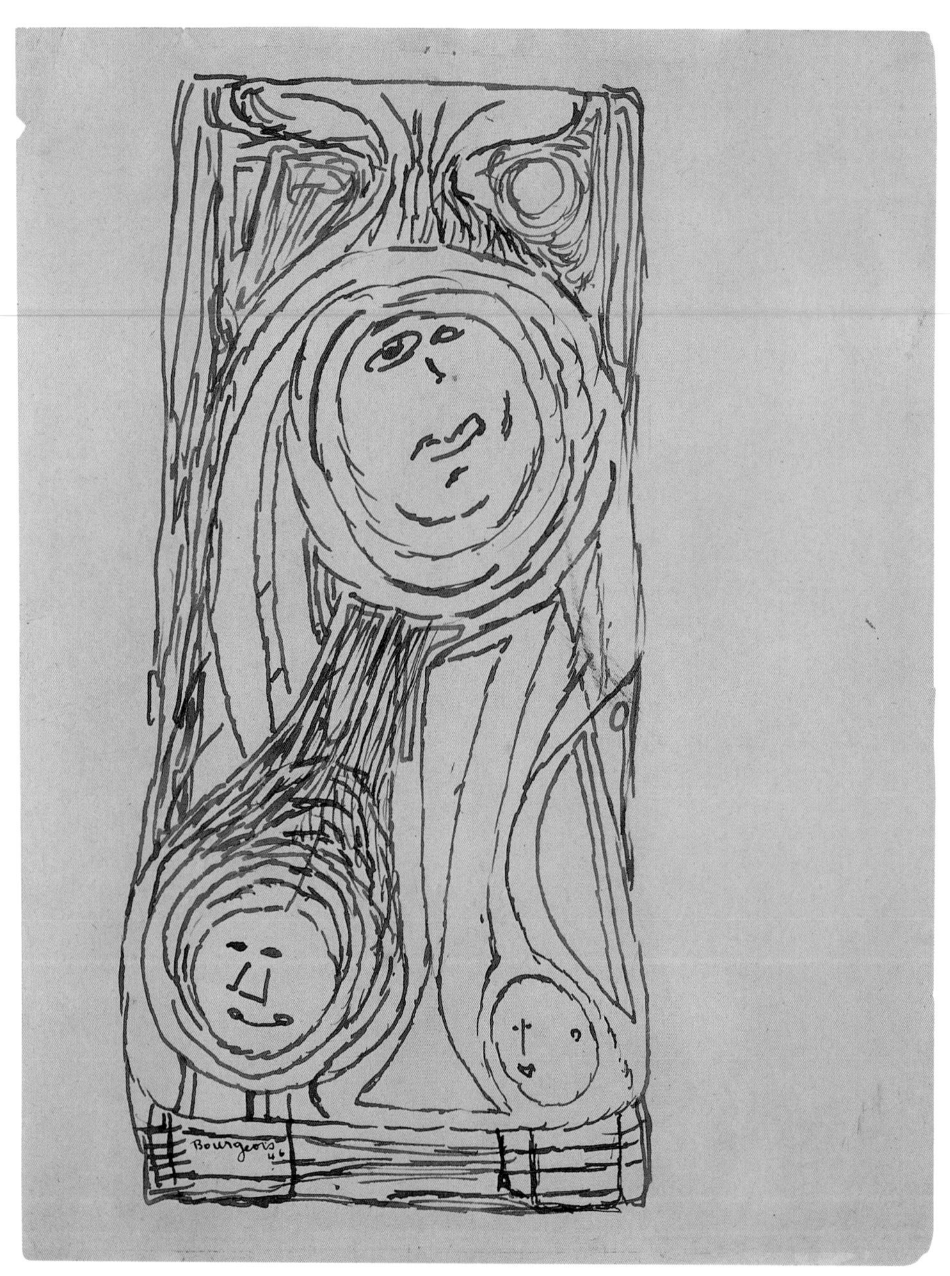

UNTITLED
Ink on paper,
1946
no. 46

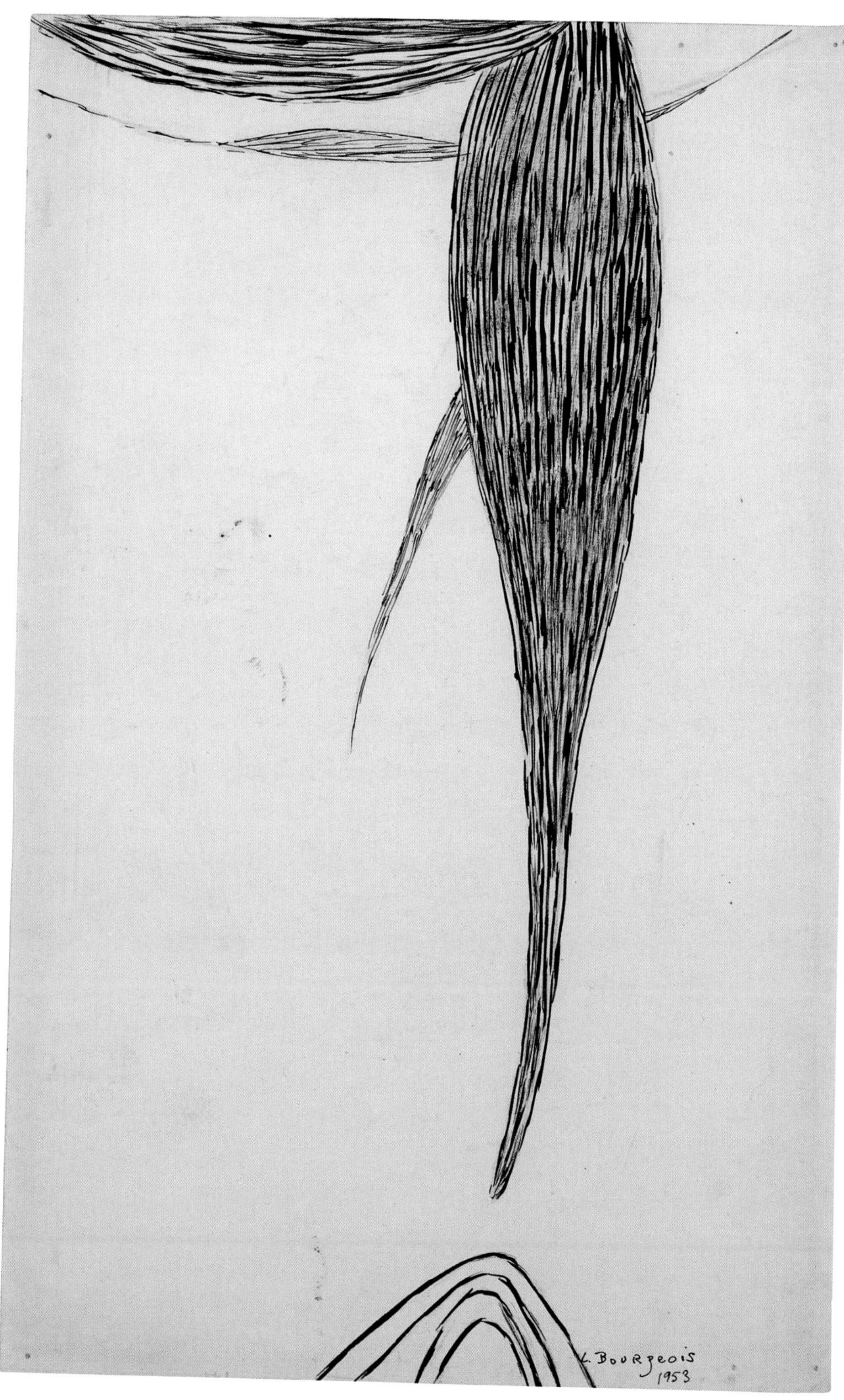

UNTITLED
Ink on paper,
1953
no. 73

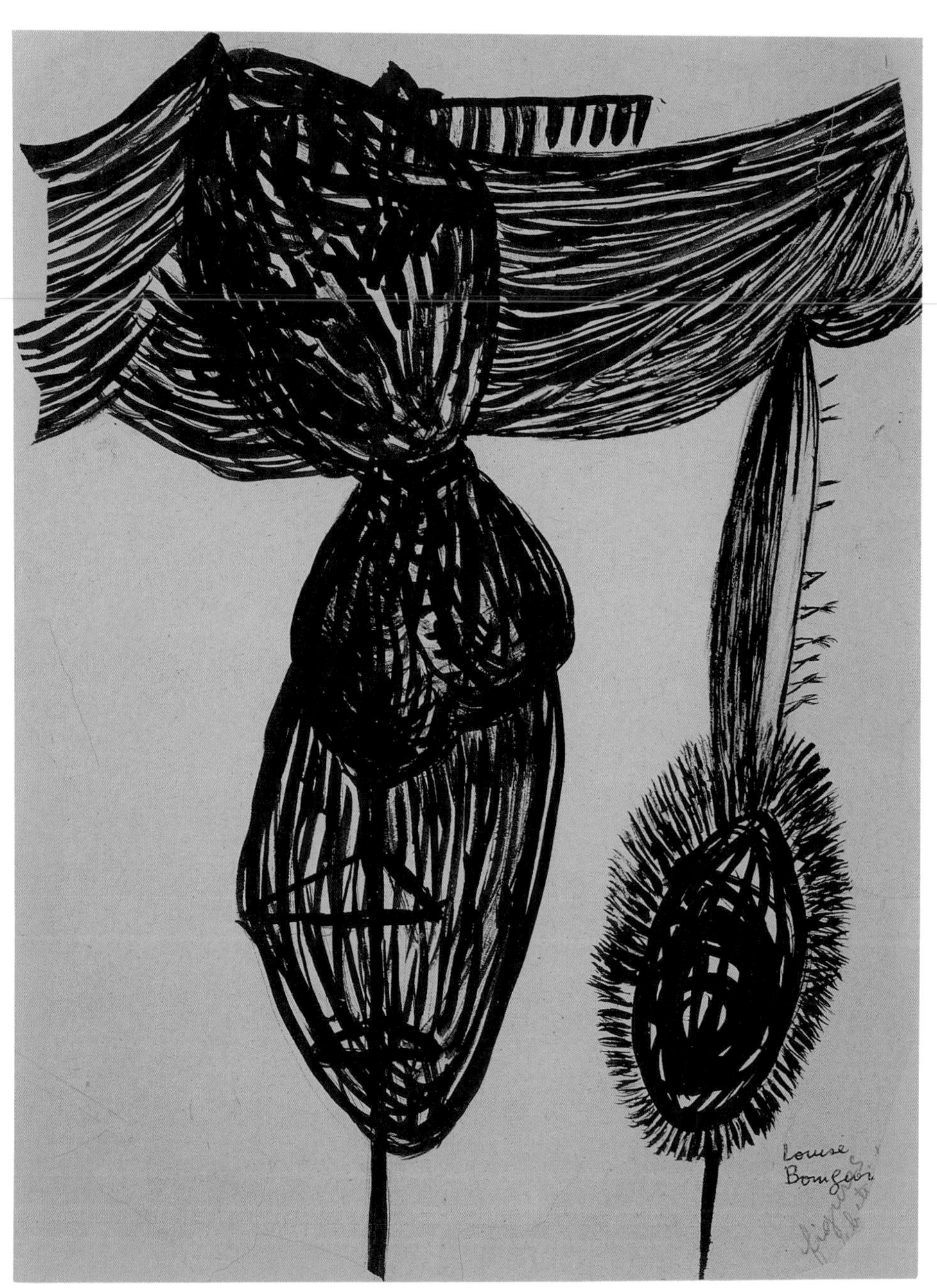

UNTITLED
Ink on tan paper,
1947
no. 48

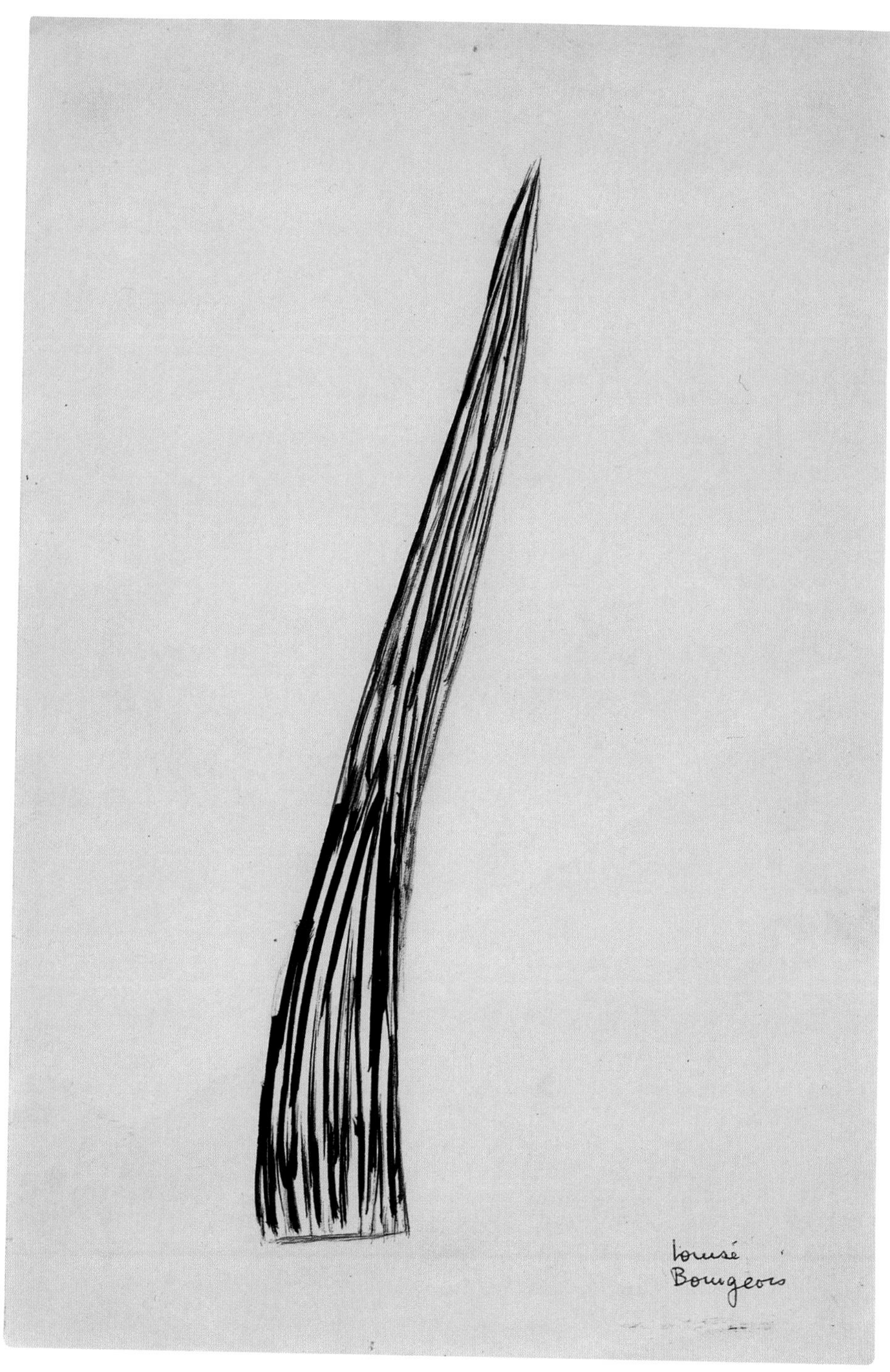

UNTITLED
Ink on paper,
1947
no. 49

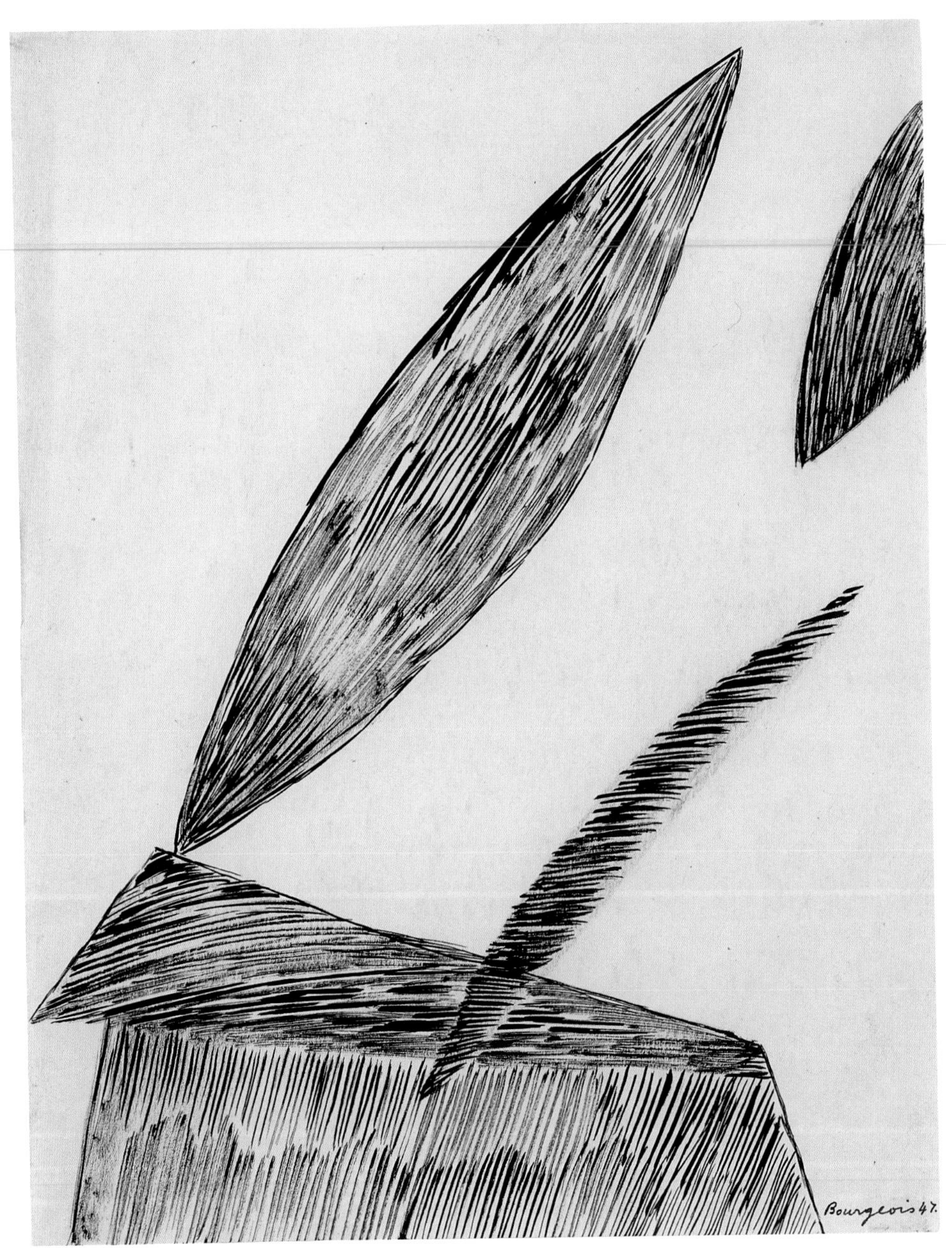

UNTITLED
Ink on paper,
1947
no. 50

UNTITLED
Pencil on paper, 1947
no. 51

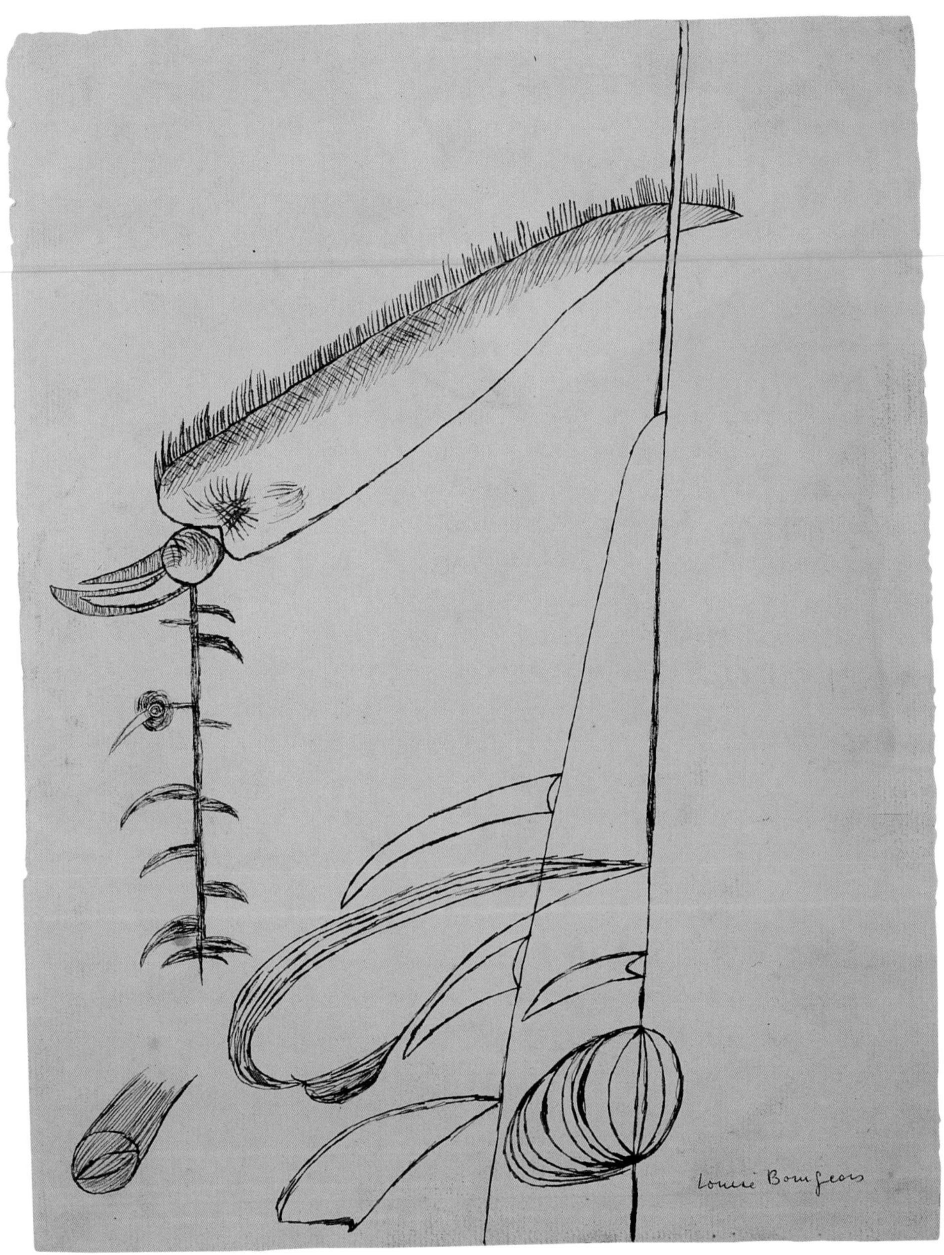

UNTITLED
Ink on paper,
1947
no. 52

UNTITLED
Brown ink on paper, 1947
no. 53

UNTITLED
Red and black ink
on paper, 1947

no. 55

UNTITLED
Ink and charcoal on paper, 1947–49
no. 56

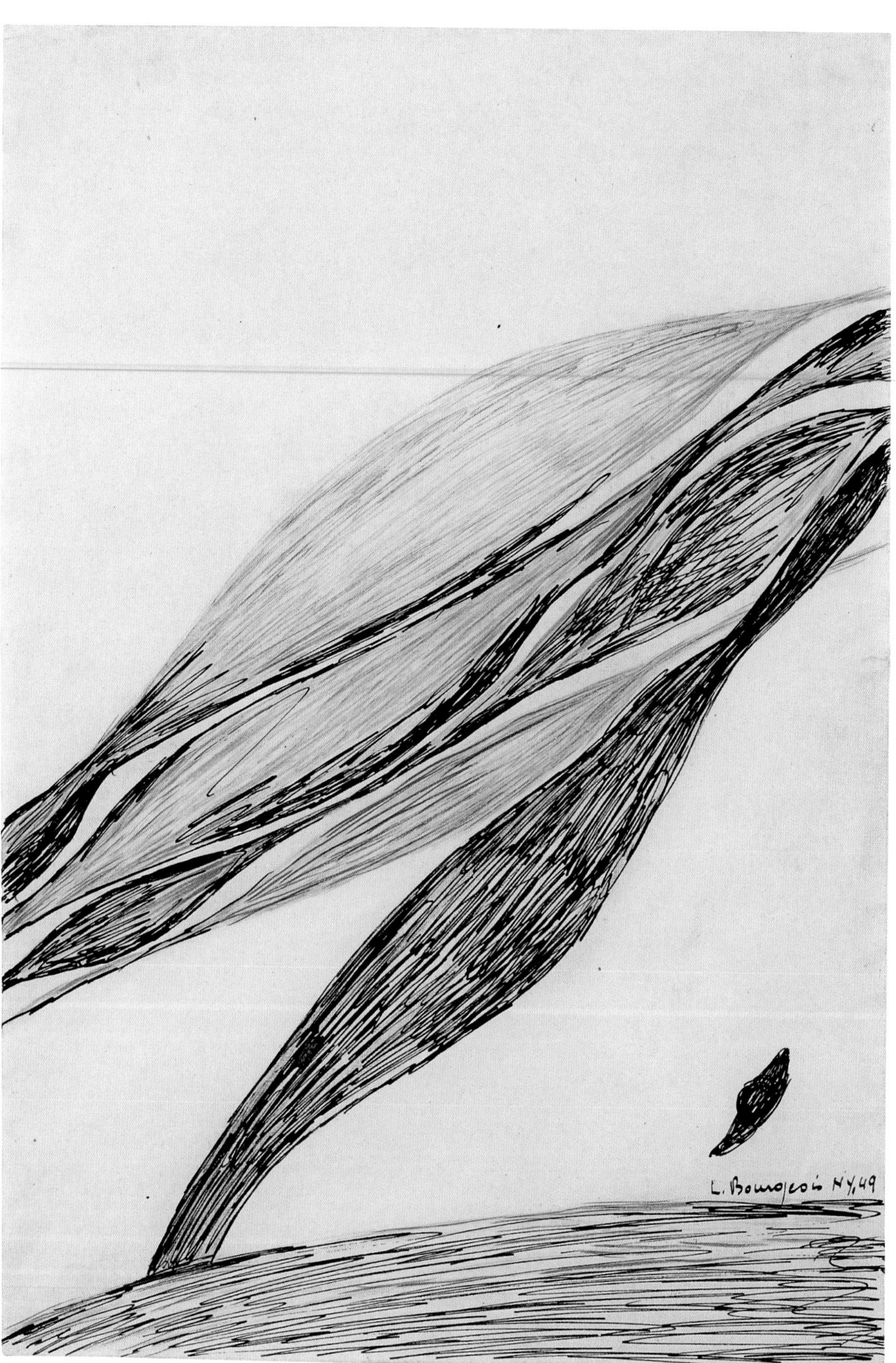

UNTITLED
Ink and pencil
on paper, 1949
no. 57

UNTITLED
Ink on paper,
1949
no. 58

UNTITLED
Pencil on newsprint, 1947
no. 54

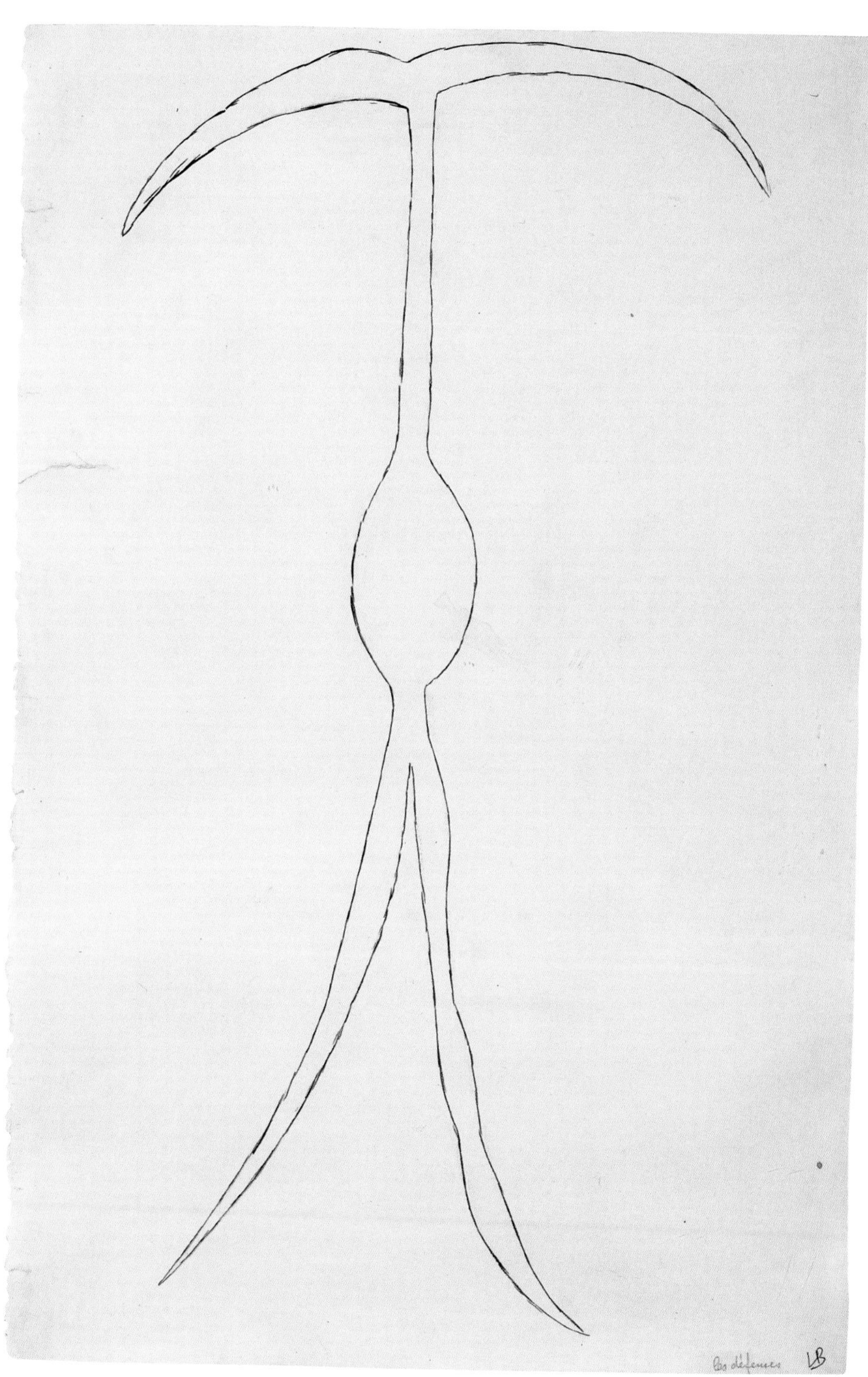

LES DEFENSES
Ink on pink
paper, 1949
no. 60

UNTITLED (VERSO & RECTO)
Ink, pencil and crayon on graph paper, 1950
no. 66

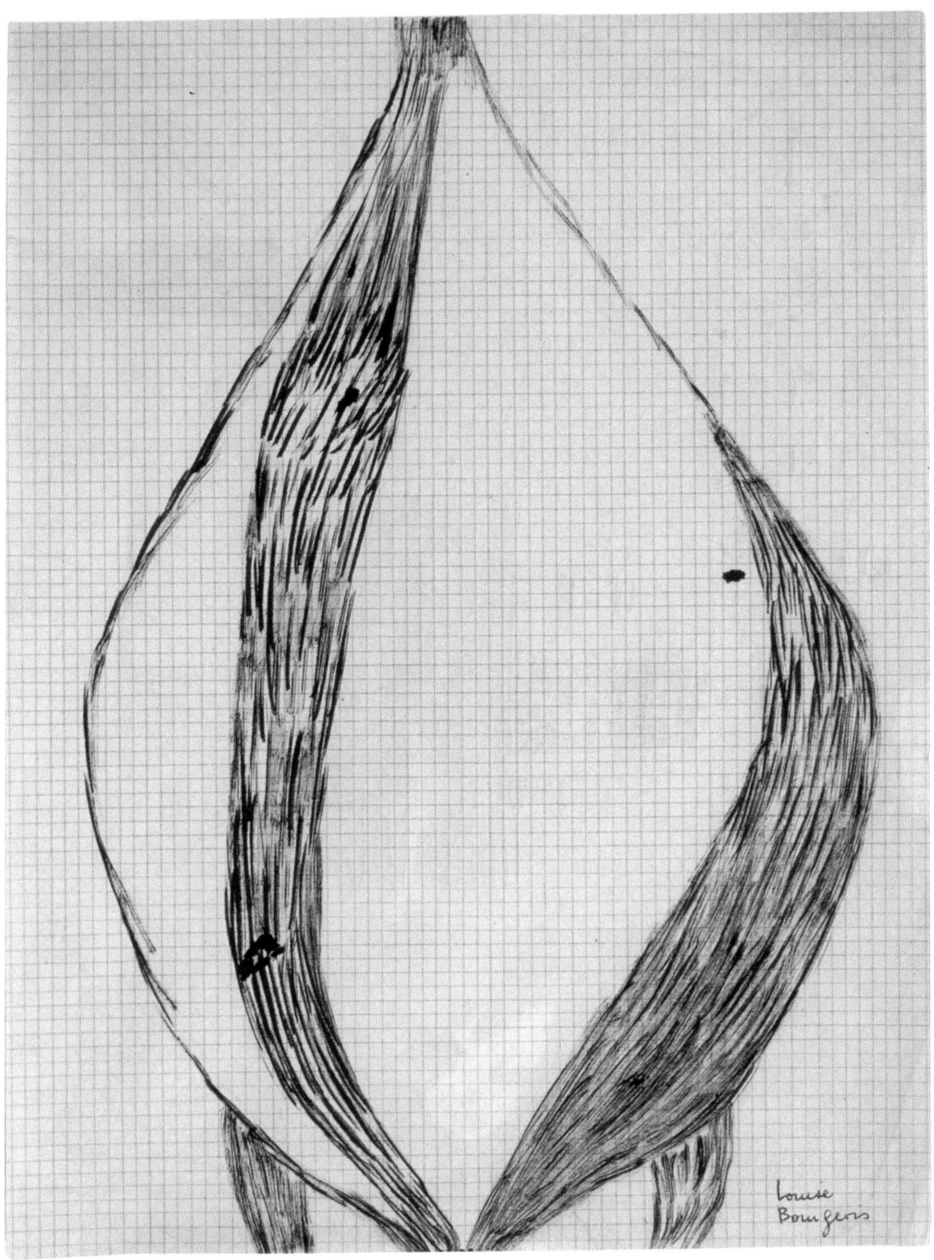
Louise
Bourgeois

LES VOLEUSES DE GRATTE CIEL
Pencil on paper, 1949
no. 62

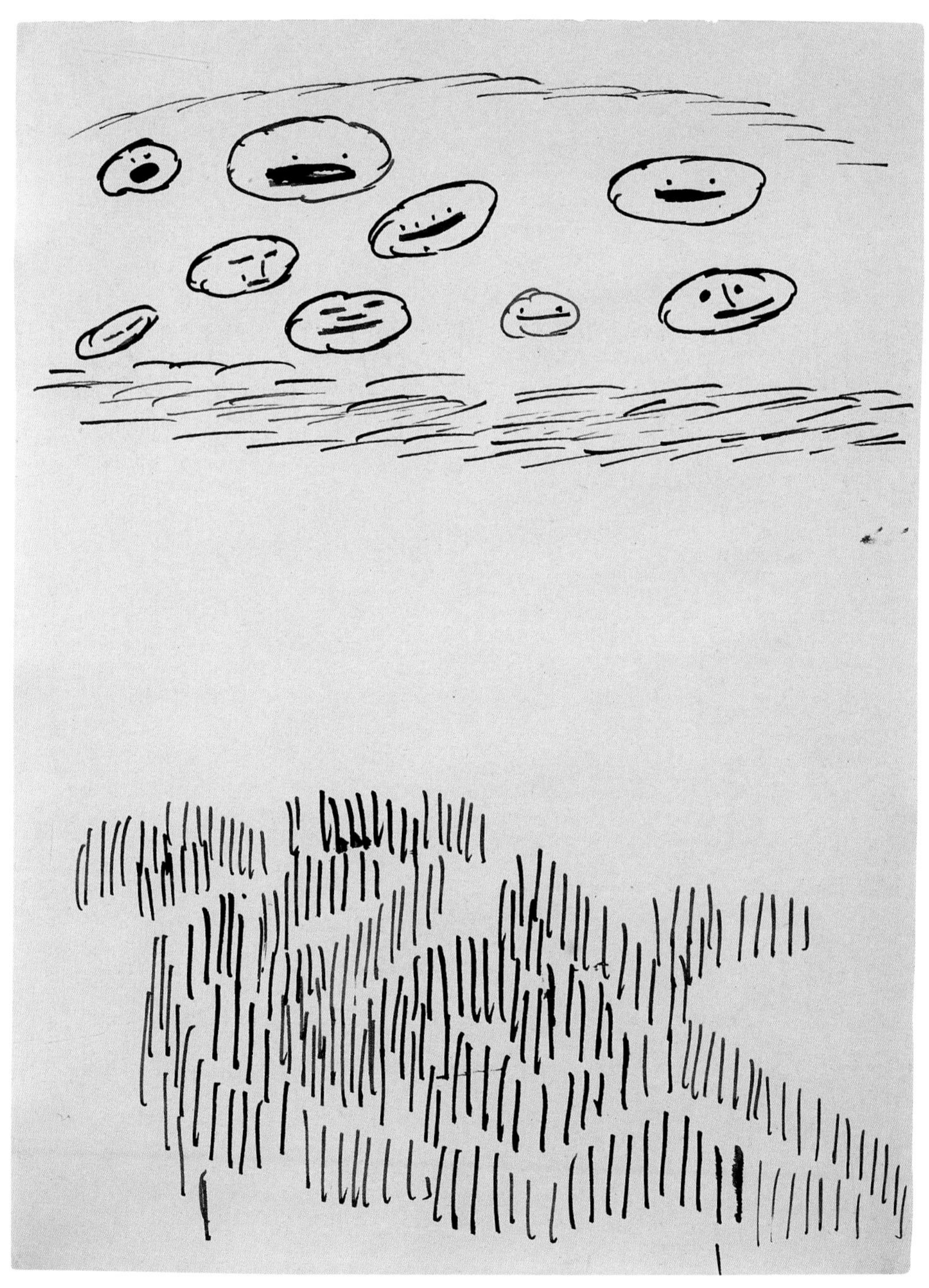

UNTITLED
Ink on paper,
1949
no. 63

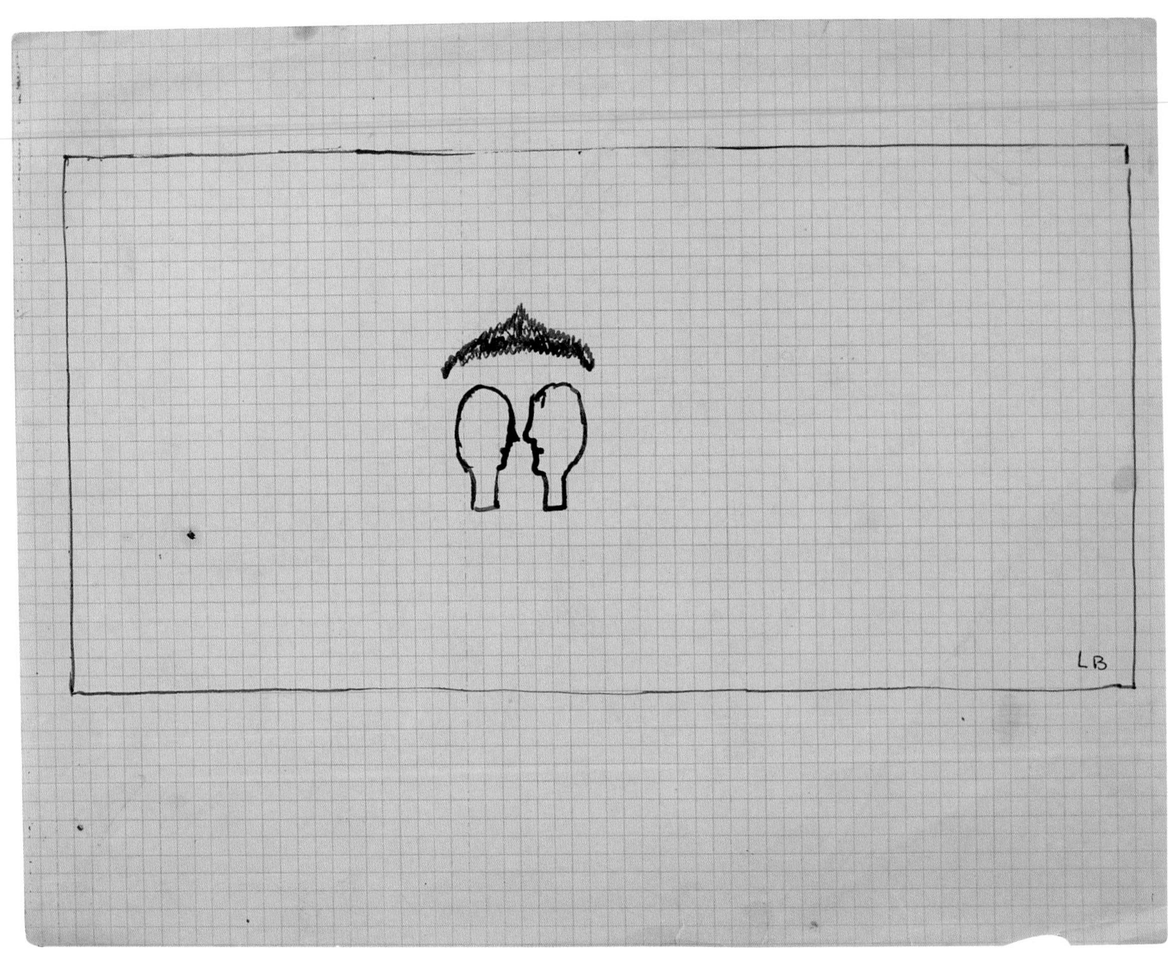

UNTITLED
Ink on graph
paper, 1947
no. 47

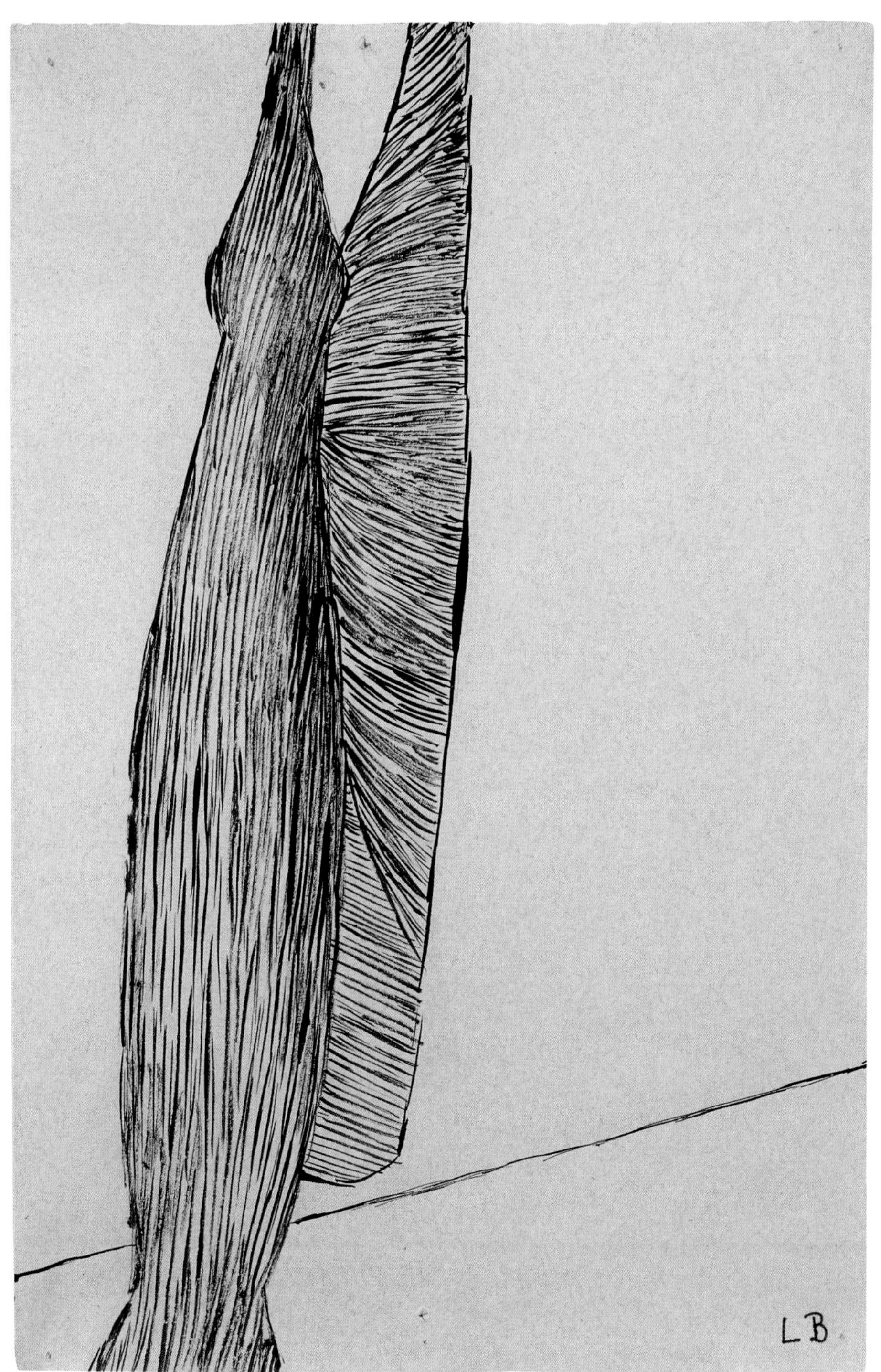

UNTITLED
Ink on paper,
1949
no. 61

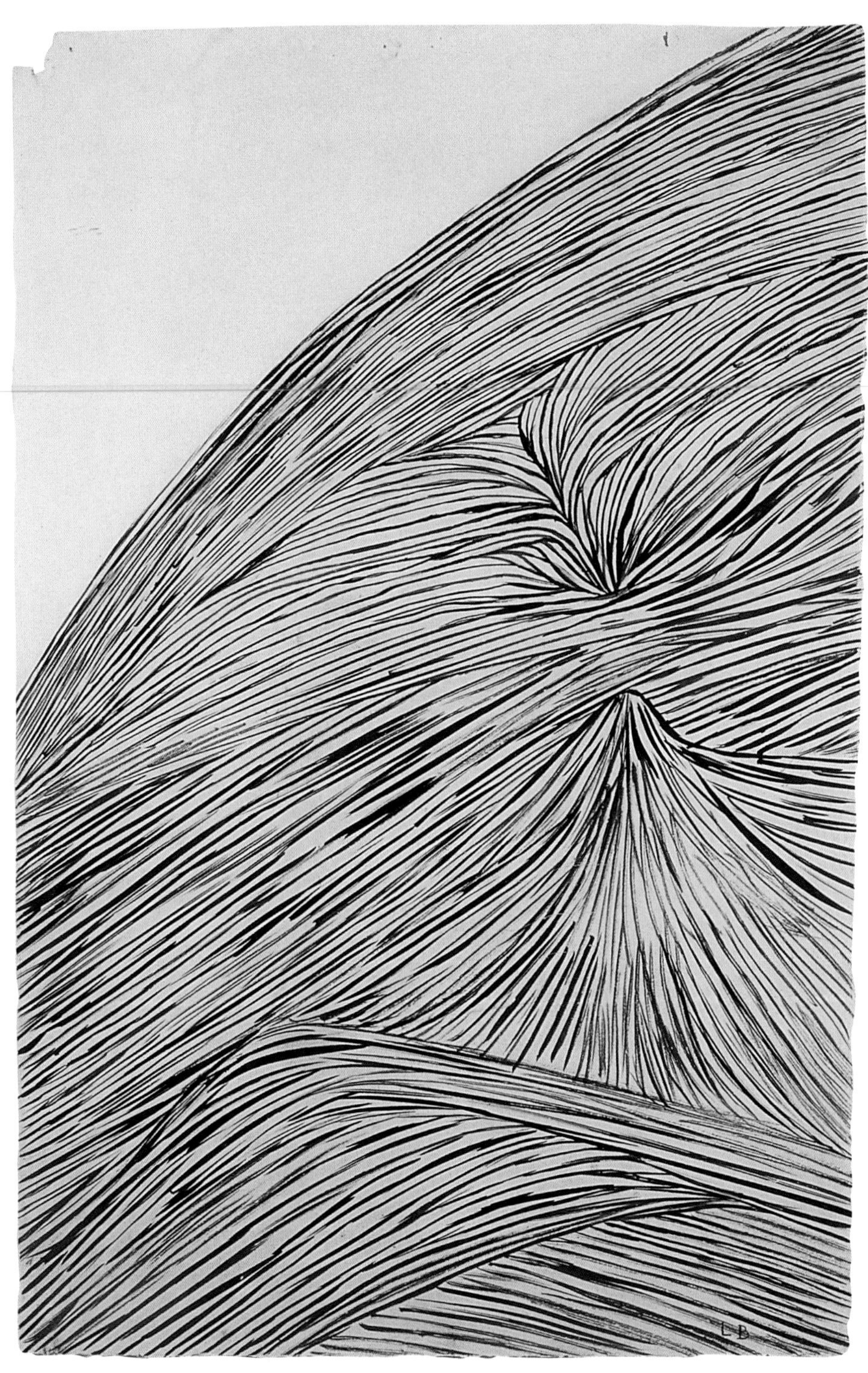

UNTITLED
Ink on paper,
1950
no. 69

UNTITLED
Ink on paper,
1949
no. 64

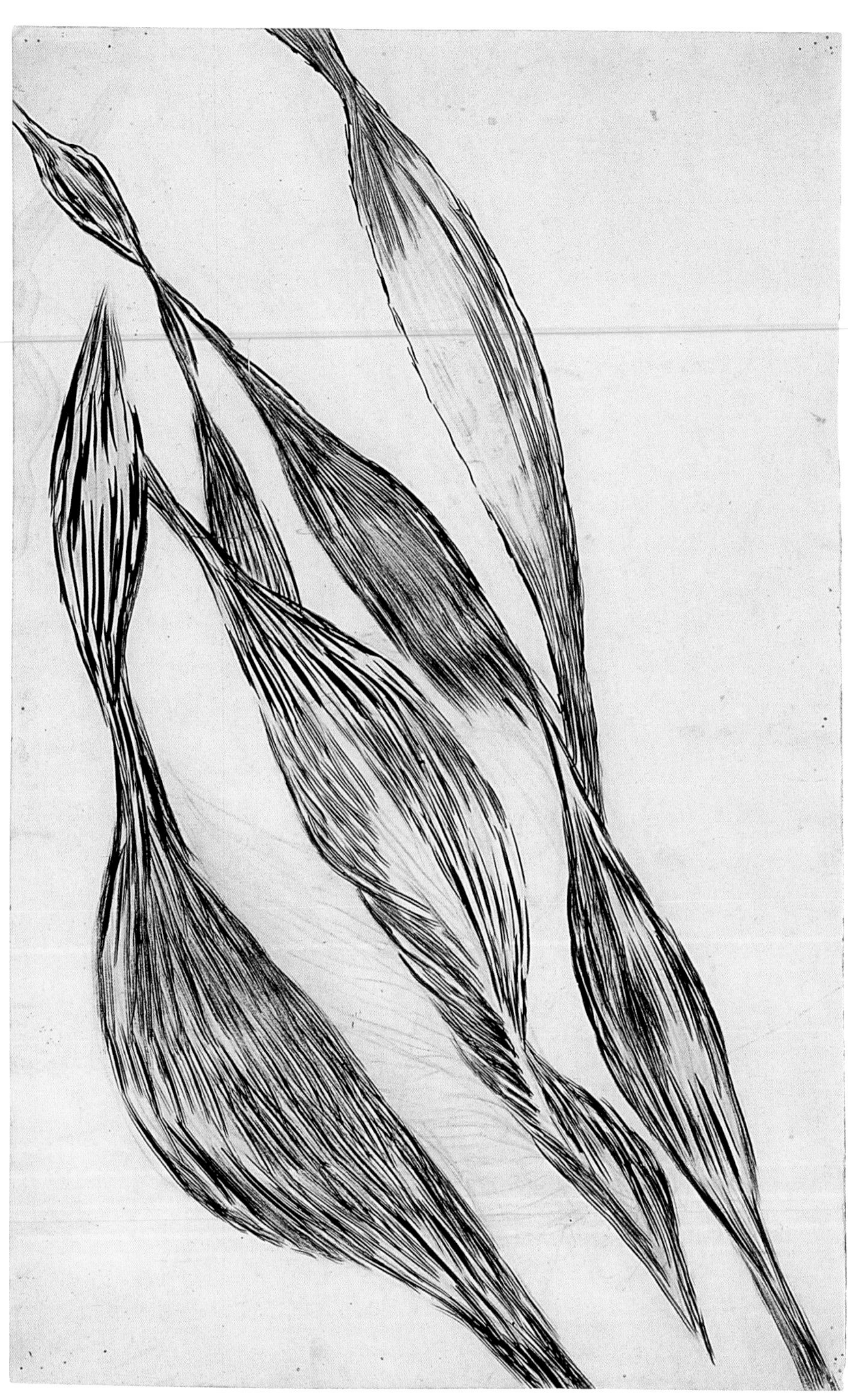

UNTITLED
Ink on paper,
1949
no. 59

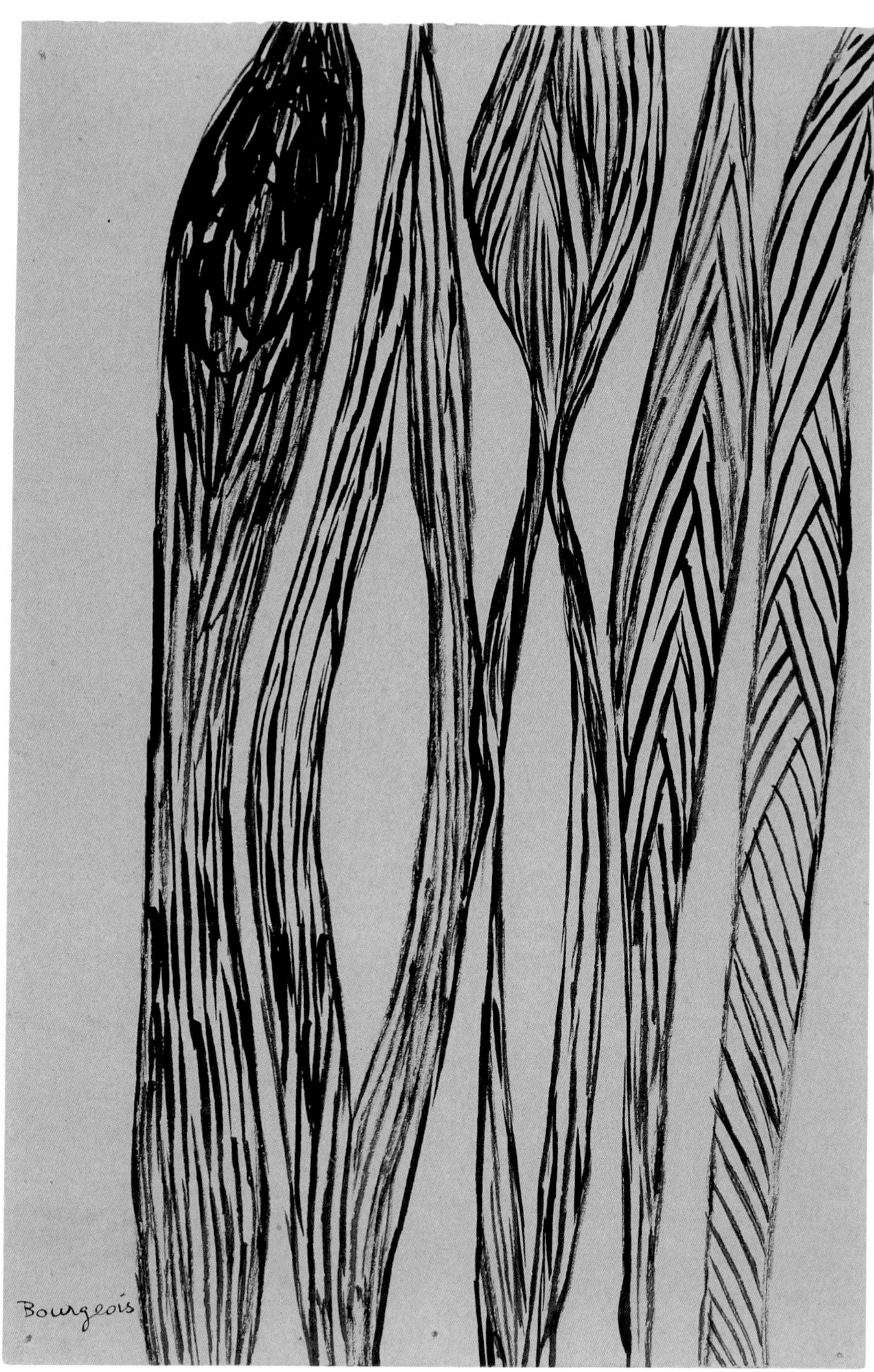

UNTITLED
Ink on paper,
1951
no. 70

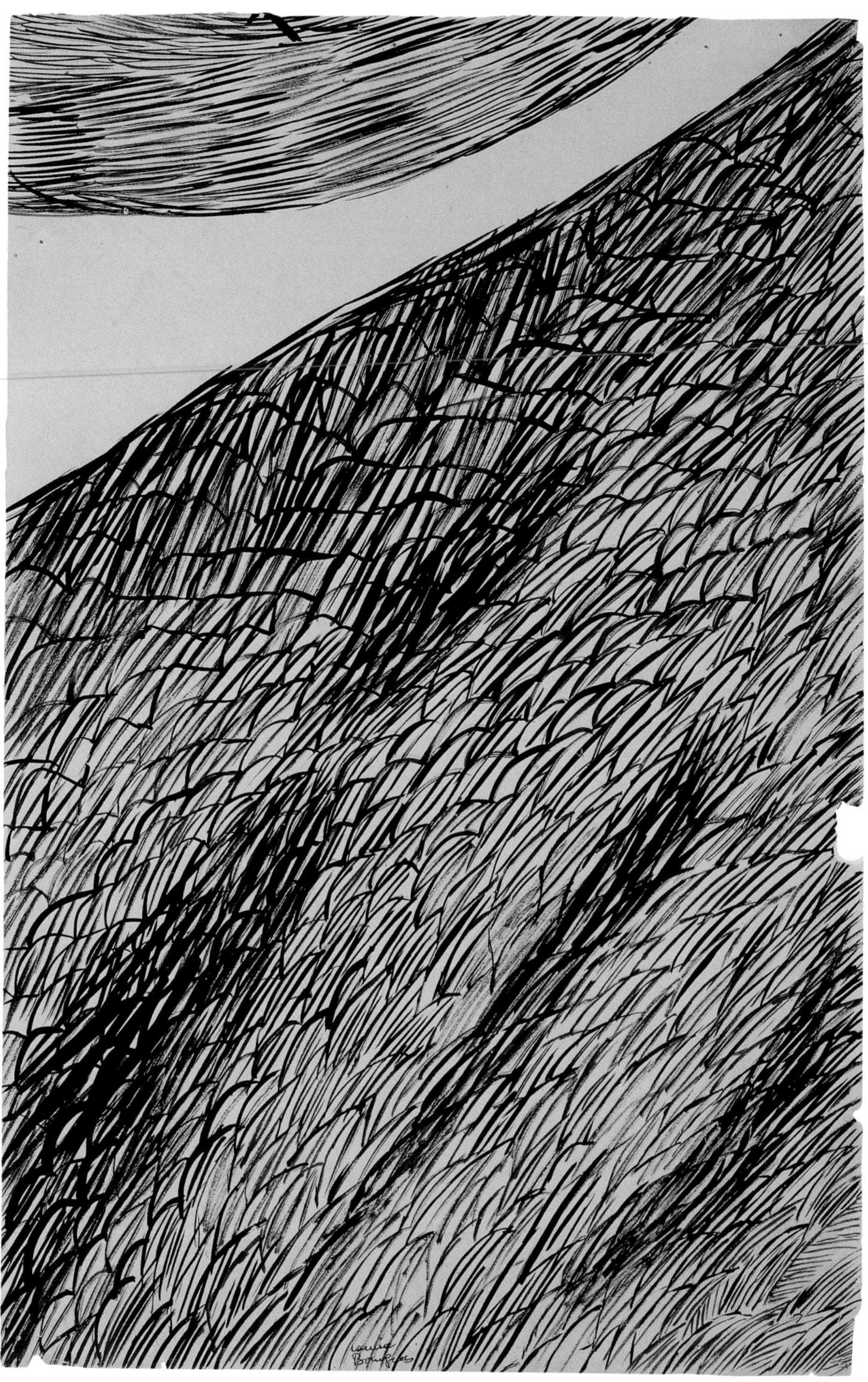

UNTITLED
Ink on paper,
1950
no. 68

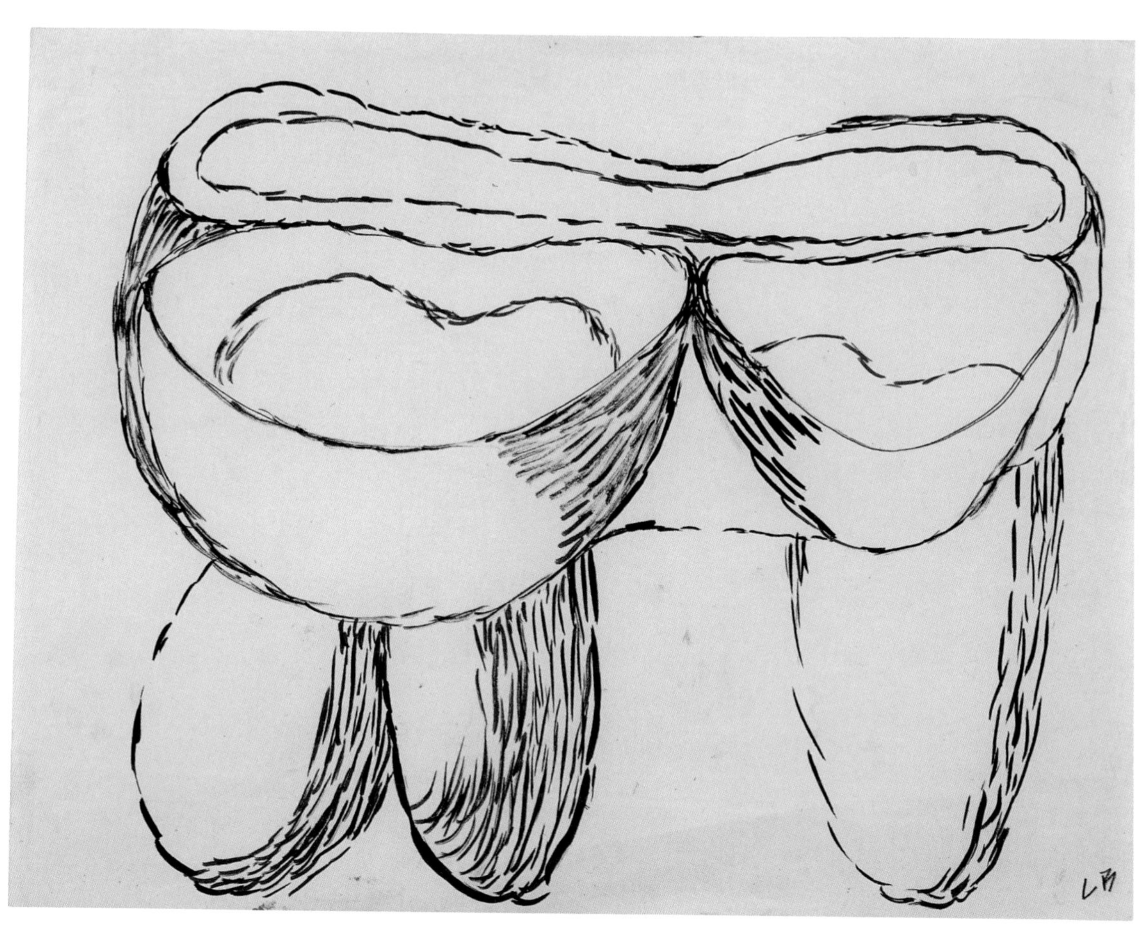

UNTITLED
Ink on paper,
1953
no. 72

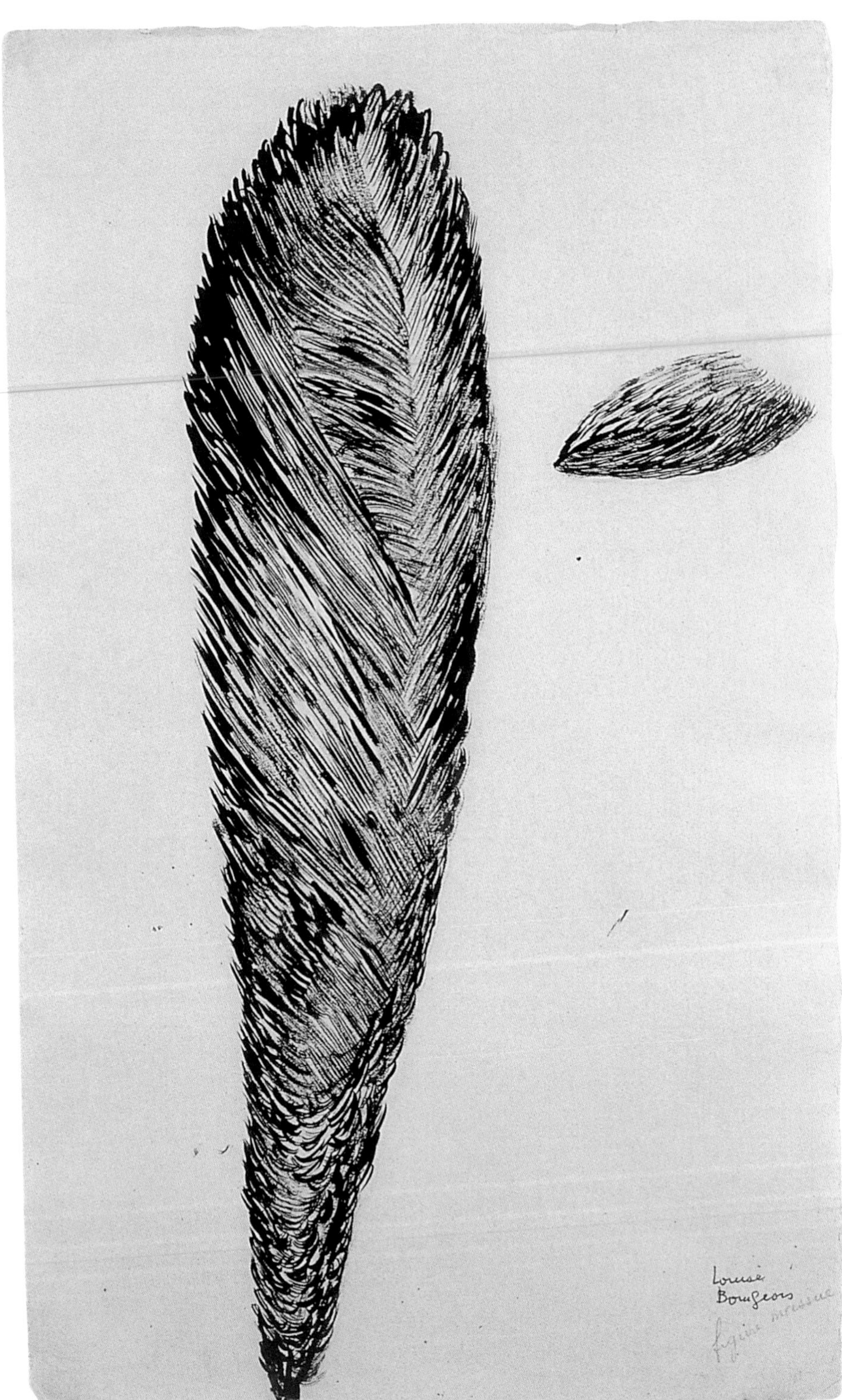

FIGURE MASSUE
Ink on paper,
1949
no. 65

UNTITLED
Ink on paper,
1951
no. 71

list of works

All works from the collection of the artist are courtesy of Cheim & Read, New York.

PAINTINGS

1. *Reparation*, 1938–40
Oil on linen
30 × 20 in; 76.2 × 50.8 cm
Collection of the artist

2. *Untitled*, 1945
Oil on canvas
40 ¼ × 24 in; 102.1 × 61 cm
Peter Blum Gallery, New York

3. *Untitled*, 1946
Oil on canvas
44 × 22 in; 111.7 × 55.8 cm
Collection of the artist

4. *One Way Traffic*, 1946
Oil on canvas
36 × 14 in; 91.4 × 35.6 cm
Collection of the artist

5. *Untitled*, 1946
Oil and chalk on canvas
44 × 22 in; 111.7 × 55.8 cm
Collection of the artist

6. *Untitled*, 1946
Oil, charcoal and pastel on canvas
36 × 24 ⅛ in;
91.4 × 61.3 cm
Collection of the artist

7. *Untitled*, 1946–47
Oil on linen
36 × 14 in; 91.4 × 35.6 cm
Collection of the artist

8. *Untitled*, 1946–47
Oil on canvas
26 × 44 in; 66 × 111.7 cm
Ginny Williams Family Foundation, Collection of Ginny Williams, Denver

9. *Untitled*, 1946–47
Oil on wood
11 ½ × 32 in; 29.2 × 81.3 cm
Collection of the artist

10. *It is Six Fifteen*, 1946–48
Oil on canvas
36 × 24 in; 91.4 × 35.6 cm
Collection of the artist

11. *Regrettable Incident in the Louvre Palace*, 1947
Oil on canvas
14 ⅛ × 36 in;
35.9 × 91.4 cm
Collection of the artist

12. *Untitled*, 1947
Oil on canvas
44 × 26 in; 111.8 × 66 cm
Collection of the artist

13. *Untitled*, 1948
Oil on canvas
60 × 30 in; 152.4 × 76.2 cm
Ginny Williams Family Foundation, Collection of Ginny Williams, Denver

14. *Woman in Process of Placing a Beam in Her Bag*, 1948
Oil on canvas
44 × 25 ¾ in;
111.8 × 65.4 cm
Collection of the artist

15. *No Swearing Allowed*, 1949
Oil on canvas
56 × 15 in; 142.2 × 38.1 cm
Collection of the artist

PRINTS

16. *He Disappeared into Complete Silence*, 1947
Suite of 9 engravings with text. Double-page spread,
10 × 14 in; 25.4 × 35.6 cm
Collection of the artist

17. *The Puritan*
Suite of 8 engravings with text, hand painted.
Text: 1947, prints: 1990
Linen covered portfolio,
27 ¼ × 20 ¾ × 2 in;
69.2 × 52.7 × 5.8 cm
Collection of the artist
(Not reproduced in catalogue)

SCULPTURES *(PERSONAGES)*

18. *The Three Graces*, 1947
Bronze, painted white
81 × 25 × 12 in;
205.7 × 63.5 × 30.5 cm
Collection of the artist

19. *Listening One*, 1947
Bronze, painted white
80 × 20 × 12 in;
203.2 × 50.8 × 30.5 cm
Collection of the artist

20. *Paddle Woman*, 1947
Bronze
57 ¾ × 16 ¼ × 12 in;
146.6 × 41.2 × 30.4 cm
Collection of the artist

21. *Dagger Child*, 1947–49
Bronze
75 ⅝ × 12 × 12 in;
192.1 × 30.5 × 30.5 cm
Collection of the artist

22. *Needle Woman*, 1947–49
Bronze, painted white
56 ½ × 12 × 12 in;
143.5 × 30.5 × 30.5 cm
Collection of the artist

23. *Portrait of Jean-Louis*, 1947–49
Bronze, painted white and blue
35 × 5 × 4 in;
88.9 × 12.7 × 10.2 cm
Collection of the artist

24. *Black Flames*, 1947–49
Bronze
69 ½ × 12 × 12 in;
176.5 × 30.5 × 30.5 cm
Collection of the artist

25. *Portrait of C.Y.*, 1947–49
Bronze, painted white, and nails
66 ½ × 12 × 12 in;
168.9 × 30.5 × 30.5 cm
Collection of the artist

26. *Corner Piece*, 1947–49
Bronze and paint
84 × 12 × 12 in;
213.4 × 30.5 × 30.5 cm
Collection of the artist

27. *The Blind Leading the Blind*, 1947–49
Bronze, dark patina
69 ¼ × 69 × 23 in;
175.9 × 175.3 × 58.4 cm
Collection of the artist

28. *Pregnant Woman I*, 1947–49
Bronze
48 × 12 × 12 in;
121.9 × 30.5 × 30.5 cm
Collection of the artist

29. *The Winged Figure*, 1948
Bronze and paint
70 ½ × 37 ½ × 12 in;
179.1 × 95.3 × 30.5 cm
Collection of the artist

30. *Woman with Packages*, 1949
Bronze, painted white
65 × 18 × 12 in;
165.1 × 45.7 × 30.5 cm
Collection of the artist

31. *Knife Couple*, 1949
Bronze
67 ½ × 12 × 12 in;
171.5 × 30.5 × 30.5 cm
Collection of the artist

32. *Pillar*, 1949-50
Bronze, painted white and blue
63 ¼ × 12 × 12 in;
160.7 × 30.5 × 30.5 cm
Collection of the artist

33. *Depression Woman*, 1949–50
Bronze, painted white
74 ½ × 12 × 12 in;
189.2 × 30.5 × 30.5 cm
Collection of the artist

34. *Friendly Evidence*, 1947–49
Bronze
70 × 12 × 12 in;
177.8 × 30.4 × 30.4 cm
Collection of the artist

35. *Untitled*, 1950
Bronze, stainless steel, and mirror
66 ½ × 12 × 12 in;
168.9 × 30.5 × 30.5 cm
Collection of the artist

36. *Mortise*, 1950
Bronze, painted red and black
55 ¾ × 18 × 18 in;
141.6 × 45.7 × 45.7 cm
Collection of the artist

37. *Memling Dawn*, 1951
Bronze
64 × 15 × 18 in;
162.6 × 38.1 × 45.7 cm
Collection of the artist

38. *Quarantania*, 1947–53
Bronze, dark patina
80 ½ × 27 × 27 in;
204.4 × 68.6 × 68.6 cm
Collection of the artist

39. *Untitled*, 1953
Bronze
59 ¼ × 8 ½ × 8 ½ in:
105.5 × 21.6 × 21.6 cm
Collection of the artist

40. *Untitled*, 1954
Painted wood
73 × 12 × 12 in;
185.4 × 30.5 × 30.5 cm
Collection of the artist

41. *One and Others*, 1955
Painted and stained wood
18 × 20 1/16 × 16 15/16 in;
45.7 × 51 × 43 cm
Whitney Museum of American Art, New York

42. *Untitled*, 1954–62
Painted wood and latex
58 × 12 × 12 in;
147.3 × 30.5 × 30.5 cm
Collection of the artist

DRAWINGS

43. *Untitled*, 1942
Pencil on paper
9 × 8 ½ in; 22.9 × 21.6 cm
Collection Jerry Gorovoy, New York

44. *Easton House*, 1946
Ink on graph paper
8 ½ × 11 in; 21.6 × 27.9 cm
Collection of the artist

45. *Untitled (double sided)*, 1946
Pencil on paper
8 ½ × 7 in; 21.6 × 17.8 cm
Collection of the artist

46. *Untitled*, 1946
Ink on paper
10 15/16 × 8 3/8 in;
27.8 × 21.3 cm
Collection of the artist

47. *Untitled*, 1947
Ink on graph paper
8 ½ × 11 in; 21.6 × 27.9 cm
Collection of the artist

48. *Untitled*, 1947
Ink on tan paper
10 ¾ × 8 ¼ in;
27.3 × 21 cm
Collection of the artist

49. *Untitled*, 1947
Ink on paper
10 ½ × 7 1/8 in;
26.7 × 18.1 cm
Collection of the artist

50. *Untitled*, 1947
Ink on paper
11 × 8 ½ in; 27.9 × 21.6 cm
Collection of the artist

51. *Untitled*, 1947
Pencil on paper
7 ¼ × 5 1/8 in;
18.4 × 13 cm
Collection of the artist

52. *Untitled*, 1947
Ink on paper
12 3/8 × 9 ½ in;
31.4 × 24.1 cm
Collection of the artist

53. *Untitled*, 1947
Brown ink on paper
11 ½ × 7 3/8 in;
29.2 × 18.7 cm
Collection of the artist

54. *Untitled*, 1947
Pencil on newsprint
8 × 5 in; 20.3 × 12.7 cm
Collection of the artist

55. *Untitled*, 1947
Red and black ink on paper
10 ¾ × 8 ¾ in;
27.3 × 22.2 cm
Collection of the artist

56. *Untitled*, 1947-49
Ink and charcoal on paper
11 ¾ × 6 3/8 in;
29.8 × 16.2 cm
Collection of the artist

57. *Untitled*, 1949
Ink and pencil on paper
10 ½ × 7 ¼ in;
26.7 × 18.4 cm
Collection of the artist

58. *Untitled*, 1949
Ink on paper
8 ½ × 11 in; 21.6 × 27.9 cm
Collection of the artist

59. *Untitled*, 1949
Ink on paper
12 3/8 × 6 ¼ in;
31.4 × 15.9 cm
The Art Collection of Bank One, Chicago

60. *Les Defenses*, 1949
Ink on pink paper
20 × 13 in; 50.8 × 33 cm
Collection of the artist

61. *Untitled*, 1949
Ink on paper
8 × 5 ¼ in; 20.3 × 13.3 cm
Collection of the artist

62. *Les Voleuses de Gratte Ciel*, 1949
Pencil on paper
8 × 5 in; 20.3 × 12.7 cm
Collection of the artist

63. *Untitled*, 1949
Ink on paper
12 × 9 in; 30.5 × 22.9 cm
Collection of the artist

64. *Untitled*, 1949
Ink on paper
19 ¾ × 12 ¾ in;
50.2 × 32.4 cm
Peter Blum Gallery, New York

65. *Figure Massue*, 1949
Ink on paper
15 ½ × 9 ½ in;
39.4 × 24.1 cm
Peter Blum Gallery, New York

66. *Untitled (verso and recto)*, 1950
Ink, pencil, and crayon on graph paper
11 × 8 ½ in; 27.9 × 21.6 cm
Collection of the artist

67. *Untitled*, 1950
Ink on paper
11 ½ × 9 ¾ in;
29.2 × 24.8 cm
Collection of the artist
(Not reproduced in catalogue)

68. *Untitled*, 1950
Ink on paper
19 × 12 ½ in;
48.3 × 31.8 cm
Collection of the artist

69. *Untitled*, 1950
Ink on paper
19 × 12 ½ in; 48.3 × 31.8 cm
Peter Blum Gallery,
New York

70. *Untitled*, 1951
Ink on paper
8 ⅛ × 5 ⅜ in; 20.6 × 13.7 cm
Collection of the artist

71. *Untitled*, 1951
Ink on paper
22 ½ × 14 ¼ in:
57.2 × 36.2 cm
The Art Collection of
Bank One, Chicago

72. *Untitled*, 1953
Ink on paper
8 ½ × 11 in; 21.6 × 27.9 cm
Collection of the artist

73. *Untitled*, 1953
Ink on paper
11 ½ × 7 ¼ in;
29.2 × 18.4 cm
Collection of the artist

chronology

1911
Louise Joséphine Bourgeois is born in Paris on December 25 to Louis and Joséphine Bourgeois.

1912
The Bourgeois family rents a large, mid-nineteenth century house in Choisy-le-Roi outside of Paris where they will live until 1917. Behind the house is a two-story atelier for the workers in the family's tapestry business.

1915–1918
Louis Bourgeois fights in World War I. As a result of the war, the family moves to Aubusson. The Bourgeois family acquires a property in Antony that includes a house, a rear atelier, a hothouse, and gardens that are separated by the banks of the Bièvre River.

1920
Louise, her brother Pierre (born 1913), and sister Henriette (born 1904) attend school in Antony.

1921–1927
Bourgeois attends the Collège Sévigné and the Lycée Fénélon in Paris. At the age of twelve, Bourgeois begins using her drawing skills to help out in the tapestry workshop. She draws in the sections of the missing parts that are to be restored. Since it was often the bottoms of the tapestries that were in the worst state of disrepair, Bourgeois became an expert at drawing legs and feet. This imagery recurs throughout her entire body of work.

1921
Just after World War I, Bourgeois' mother contracts the Spanish flu. Bourgeois' education is intermittently interrupted so that she can care for her mother.

1922
Sadie Gordon Richmond is hired by Bourgeois' father to teach English to the Bourgeois children. Sadie lives with the Bourgeois family periodically until 1932. During this time she becomes Louis Bourgeois' mistress.

1923–1928
The Bourgeois family rents the Villa Marcel in Le Cannet. They spend the winters at Le Cannet and summers at Antony. Bourgeois attends the Lycée International in Cannes. Louise and her mother become acquainted with Pierre Bonnard.

1925
Bourgeois visits the celebrated *Le Salon des Arts Décoratifs et Industriels Modernes* exposition where she sees the Pavillion de L'Afrique Française and Le Corbusier's Pavillion de L'Esprit Nouveau. She also encounters the works of Frederick Kiesler and Vladimir Tatlin.

1929
Bourgeois travels to England.

1930
Bourgeois continues to study English at the Berlitz School in Nice and continues her education by correspondence at the Ecole Universelle in mathematics, physics, and chemistry.

1932
Bourgeois enters the Sorbonne briefly to study calculus and geometry, receiving the Baccalauréat in Philosophy from the University of Paris. Her disseratation is on Blaise Pascal and Emmanuel Kant. She travels to Russia. Louise's mother Joséphine dies on September 14 in Antony.

1933–1938
Bourgeois begins to pursue art. Over the next several years, she studies in various artists' ateliers in Montparnasse and Montmartre. In 1934 she makes a second trip to Russia, this time to see the Moscow Theater and work of the Russian Constructivists. In the years 1936–38, Bourgeois studies at the Académie de la Grande-Chaumière. She also studies under Marcel Gromaire, André Lhote, and Fernand Léger.

1936
Bourgeois rents her first apartment at 31 rue de Seine. From May 1937

through February 1938, André Breton will open and direct the gallery Gradiva in the same building.

1937–1938
Bourgeois studies art history at L'Ecole du Louvre in order to become a fully certified docent at the Louvre.

1938
Bourgeois partitions off part of her father's space at 174 Boulevard Saint-Germain to open up her own art gallery dealing in prints and paintings by Delacroix, Matisse, Redon, Valadon, and Bonnard. There she meets Robert Goldwater, an American art historian who is in Paris doing further research on his doctoral thesis "Primitivism in Modern Painting." Goldwater and Bourgeois marry on September 12 in Paris.

1938
Bourgeois moves to New York City with Goldwater. They live at 63 Park Avenue.

1939–1945
Bourgeois enrolls at the Art Students League in New York City, studying with Vaclav Vytlacil. She begins making prints. Throughout the 1940s and 1950s, because of Goldwater's position as professor of art history and editor, Bourgeois circulates within a world of art historians that includes Alfred Barr, Clement Greenberg, Erwin Panofsky, Meyer Shapiro, and James Johnson Sweeney, among others. They also socialize with American artists such as Willem de Kooning, Franz Kline, Louise Nevelson, Maurice Prendergast, and Mark Rothko, and European artists like André Breton, Marcel Duchamp, Fernand Léger, Piet Mondrian, and Le Corbusier.

1939
Bourgeois and Goldwater move to 333 East 41st Street, where they will live for two years. They return to France to arrange for

documents france 1940-1944
art - literature - press of the french underground

UNDERGROUND ANTI-NAZI PRESS

its purpose was the organization of an effective resistance. its newspapers, tracts, and pamphlets were addressed to the general public, to trade unions, and to professional groups:
defense de la france
resistance
combat
le franc tireur
la revue libre
l'insurge
liberer et federer
le populaire
m.o.f.
l'humanite
le peuple syndicaliste
jeune garde
cahiers politiques
les cahiers du temoignage chretien
le palais (de justice) libre
l'universite libre
etudiants de la classe 44
l'ecole de bara
le medecin francais
appel a l'intelligence francaise
debats de l'assemblee consultative provisoire
la convention de la haye
le patriote
le patriote lyonnais
l'instituteur francais

ART

posters, le marche noir,
participez au recensement,
il compte sur vous,
liberation posters
photographs
100 photos of german occupation
paintings
pierre bonnard
pablo picasso
jean dubuffet by louis parrot
jean dubuffet by pierre seghers
letter from jean paulhan to jean dubuffet
articles by rene huyghe, jean cassou
art magazines

POETRY

louis aragon (francois la colere): Broceliande (manuscrit); le musee grevin (editions de Minuit); les yeux d'elsa; le creve-coeur.
jean cassou: 33 sonnets composes en secret (editions de minuit).
jacques decour (decourdemanche): pages choisies (editions de minuit).
pierre emanuel: combats avec tes defenseurs.
loys masson: delivrez nous du mal.
pierre seghers: le domaine public; chien de pique.
poetes prisonniers (editions de minuit).
poesie 42: pour les quatre saisons (*pierre emanuel, loys masson, andre de richaud, pierre seghers*).
poesie 44: (*paul eluard, max jacob*).

PROSE

louis aragon: le crime contre l'esprit (editions de minuit); la facon de vivre et de mourir de gabriel peri; saint pol roux ou l'espoir, temoignages.
debu-bridel: angleterre (editions de minuit).
(mortagne): le marque de l'homme (editions de minuit).
jean bruller (vercors): le silence de la mer (editions de minuit).
elsa triolet (jean le guern): l'arrestation.
jean-paul sartre: la nausee; l'homme et les choses (poesie 44).
problemes du roman (confluence).
les cahiers de la liberation (editions de minuit).
andre gide: la justice avant la charite (combat).
gertrude stein: problemes du roman.

ACKNOWLEDGMENTS

this exhibition would not have been possible without the generous cooperation of the following:
office of war information; columbia university library; french press and information service.
messrs. louis clair, marcel duchamp, peter c. rhodes, eugene sheffer.
i wish to express my sincere thanks to all of them for their kind assistance.

norlyst gallery
59 west 56
new york city 19

JUNE 4 to JUNE 19, 1945
EXHIBITION ARRANGED BY LOUISE BOURGEOIS

Invitation to "Documents France, 1940–1944: Art, Literature, Press of the French Underground," curated by Louise Bourgeois for the Norlyst Gallery, New York, 1945.

the adoption of Michel Olivier, an orphan, who was born in Margaux near Bordeaux in 1936.

1940
Jean-Louis Bourgeois is born to Bourgeois and Goldwater on July 4.

1941
The family rents 142 East 18th Street. The building is called Stuyvesant's Folly and is the oldest apartment building in New York City. The family also acquires a house in Easton, Connecticut. Alain Matthew Clement, Bourgeois and Goldwater's second son, is born on November 12.

1945
Bourgeois has her first solo show, *Paintings by Louise Bourgeois* at the Bertha Schaefer Gallery, New York City. She curates *Documents, France 1940–1944: Art-Literature-Press of the French Underground* at the Norlyst Gallery (June 4–19) with the help of Marcel Duchamp. The show includes works by Bonnard, Picasso, and Dubuffet as well as literary works by Jean-Paul Sartre, Louis Aragon, and Gertrude Stein. Bourgeois is included in a group show, entitled *The Women*, at Peggy Guggenheim's Art of This Century Gallery in New York City. She exhibits for the first time at the Whitney Museum of American Art in the *Annual of Painting*. She will also be included in the 1946, 1947, 1948, 1951, and 1952 Annuals.

1946
In a workshop with her friends Joan Miró and Le Corbusier, Bourgeois learns about printmaking at Stanley William Hayter's Atelier 17.

1947
Bourgeois completes *He Disappeared into Complete Silence*, a suite of nine engravings accompanied by parables she wrote. Seventeen of her paintings are exhibited at Norlyst Gallery in New York City.

1949
Bourgeois' debut as a sculptor occurs at the Peridot Gallery in New York City with *Louise Bourgeois, Recent Work 1947–1949: Seventeen Standing Figures in Wood.*

1950
Her second sculpture exhibition, *Louise Bourgeois: Sculptures*, at the Peridot Gallery features fifteen *Personages*.

Bourgeois in the studio of her apartment at 142 East 18th Street, circa 1944.

1950–1951
Goldwater receives a Fulbright Scholarship (to conduct research in France) in 1950. The family returns briefly to France in 1951 and lives in Antony. They travel to London, where Bourgeois meets Francis Bacon. Bourgeois will have a studio in Paris until 1955.

1951
Bourgeois' father dies. Alfred Barr acquires *Sleeping Figure* (1950) from the Peridot Gallery for the Museum of Modern Art in New York City.

1953
Bourgeois has her third solo show at the Peridot Gallery. It is called *Louise Bourgeois: Drawings for Sculpture and Sculpture.* In June, Bourgeois, Goldwater, and the children depart for France; they visit the caves at Lascaux. Bourgeois also exhibits in the Annuals of the Whitney Museum of American Art from 1953 to 1957. During the summers of 1955, 1957, and 1959 the family returns to Paris.

1955
Bourgeois becomes an American citizen.

1958
The building Bourgeois and her family have lived in since 1941, Stuyvesant's Folly, is sold and designated to be demolished. The family moves to 435 West 22nd Street.

Invitation to Bourgeois' exhibition at the Norylst Gallery, New York, 1947.

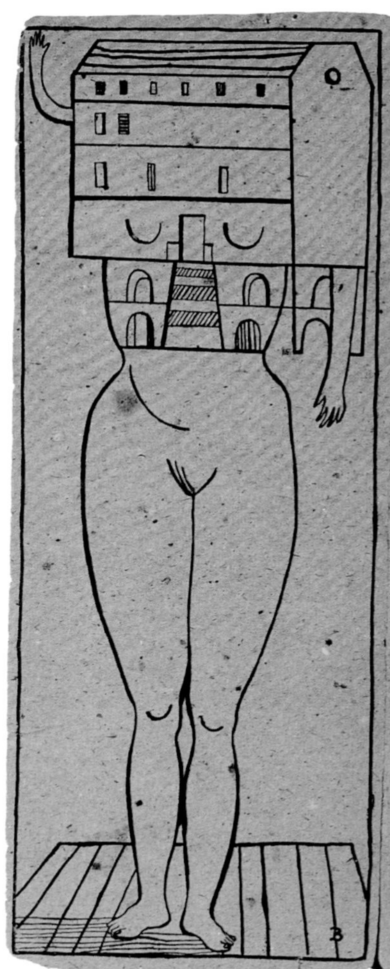

LOUISE **BOURGEOIS**

These are paintings of a city dweller . . . brown stone houses and jails . . . the bee sleeps in the dark and her domain is the sky. In her reduced geometrical space a cruel and blind life goes on . . .
·Nemecio Antunez

1 Ceremony
2 Red Night
3 Portrait
4 Game of bilboquet
5 Conversation piece
6 Jeffersonian courthouse
7 Regrettable incident in the Louvre palace
8 Processed flowers
9 Southern scene
10 Roof song
11 Two figures from a cotton mill district
12 One way traffic
13 It is six fifteen
14 Triglogue
15 Pole of joy
16 Attentive figures
17 Child asleep in a skein of wool

FROM OCTOBER 28 TO NOVEMBER 8, 1947

NORLYST GALLERY 59 WEST 56 ST. NEW YORK, N.Y.

Bourgeois opens Erasmus Books and Prints in an effort to generate more income for the family.

1960
Bourgeois teaches in the public school system in Great Neck, New York. Her work is included in the Annuals of 1960 and 1962 at the Whitney Museum of American Art in New York. Bourgeois' brother Pierre dies.

1962
The Bourgeois family moves to 347 West 20th Street, where Bourgeois still lives today.

1963
Bourgeois teaches at Brooklyn College.

1964
After eleven years without a solo show, Bourgeois exhibits a new body of work at the Stable Gallery in New York City.

1966
Bourgeois spends the summer in Europe traveling to Spain and Greece. In Barcelona she visits the Gaudí buildings. In September she is included in the exhibition *Eccentric Abstraction* organized by Lucy Lippard at the Fischbach Gallery in New York City. Her work is shown with a younger generation of artists, including Eva Hesse and Bruce Nauman.

1967–1968
Bourgeois makes her first trip to Pietrasanta, Italy, to work in marble and bronze. She will continue to return regularly to Pietrasanta through 1972. Bourgeois and Goldwater travel to Nigeria to an international symposium on African art.

1973
The marble floor piece *Number Seventy-Two (The No March)* is exhibited in the 1973 Whitney Museum of America Art's Biennial. It is subsequently acquired by Storm King Art Center in Mountainville, New York. She receives an artist's grant from the National Endowment for the Arts. Bourgeois' husband Robert Goldwater dies on March 26.

1974
Bourgeois begins teaching at the School of Visual Arts in New York City where she will teach until 1977. She also teaches at several other schools.

Bourgeois working on her sculptures, circa 1946.

1977
Bourgeois receives an Honorary Doctorate of Fine Arts degree from Yale University.

1978
Bourgeois presents the performance *A Banquet/ A Fashion Show of Body Parts. The Blind Leading the Blind* (1947) is purchased by the Detroit Institute of Art.

1980
Bourgeois travels to New Orleans to receive the Award for Outstanding Achievement in the Visual Arts at the National Women's Caucus for Art conference. She acquires her Brooklyn studio, originally a garment factory, and inherits the contents (some of which she later incorporates into her work). The studio's enormous size allows her to begin working on an unprecedented scale. Bourgeois begins a working association with Jerry Gorovoy. Bourgeois' older sister, Henriette, dies on July 9.

1981
Louise Bourgeois acquires an abandoned house in Staten Island for her son Michel. Michel never occupies the house. Bourgeois keeps it empty, turning it into a sculpture called *Maison Vide. Maison Vide* was also the title for one of Bourgeois' *Personages* from the 1940s.

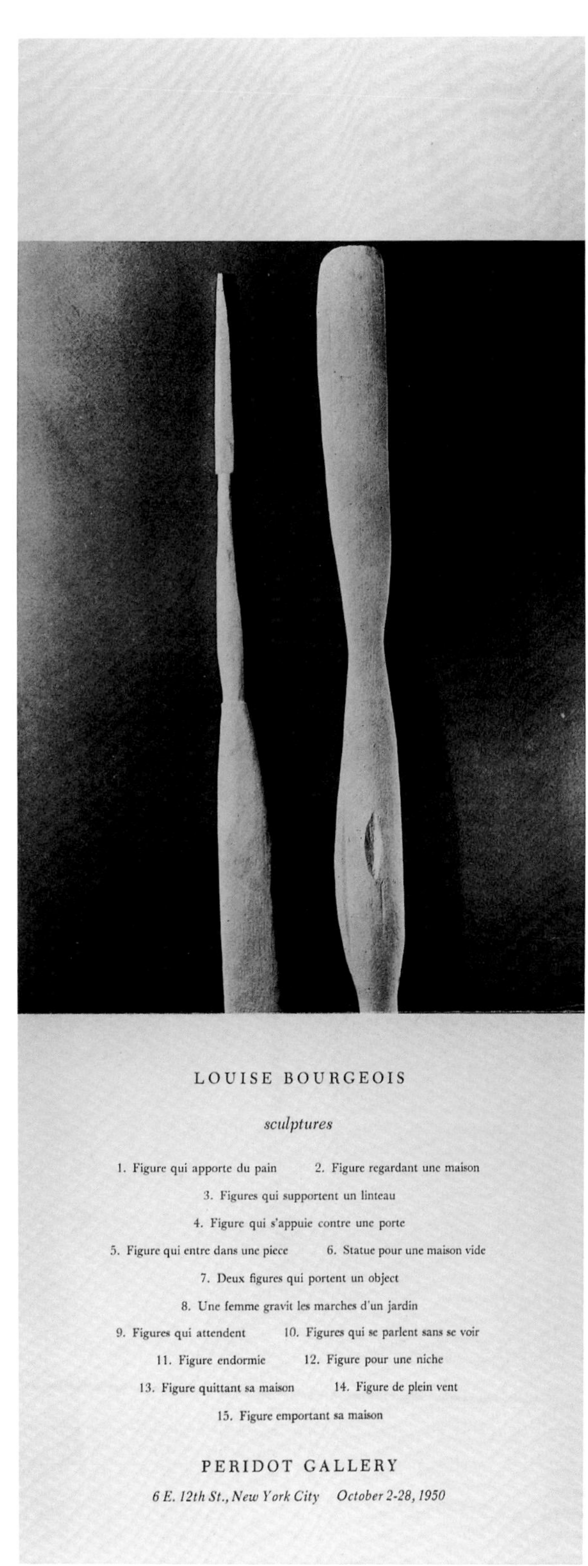

LOUISE BOURGEOIS

sculptures

1. Figure qui apporte du pain 2. Figure regardant une maison
3. Figures qui supportent un linteau
4. Figure qui s'appuie contre une porte
5. Figure qui entre dans une piece 6. Statue pour une maison vide
7. Deux figures qui portent un object
8. Une femme gravit les marches d'un jardin
9. Figures qui attendent 10. Figures qui se parlent sans se voir
11. Figure endormie 12. Figure pour une niche
13. Figure quittant sa maison 14. Figure de plein vent
15. Figure emportant sa maison

PERIDOT GALLERY

6 E. 12th St., New York City October 2-28, 1950

Invitation to Bourgeois' exhibition at the Peridot Gallery, New York, 1950: "Louise Bourgeois: Sculptures."

1982
Bourgeois' retrospective at the Museum of Modern Art in New York is the first retrospective given to a woman artist at MoMA.

1983
Bourgeois is elected a Member of the American Academy and the Institute of Arts and Letters in New York City, and receives an Honorary Doctorate of Fine Arts Degree from the Massachusetts College of Art in Boston. Jack Lang, the French Minister of Culture, awards the distinction of "Officier de L'Ordre des Arts et des Lettres" to Bourgeois.

1990
Bourgeois' son, Michel, dies.

1991
Bourgeois is awarded the Grand Prix in sculpture by the French Ministry of Culture.

1992
Peter Blum Editions publishes *Homely Girl, A Life*, a collaboration between Arthur Miller and Louise Bourgeois.

Above: Three "Spiral Women," early 1950s.

PHOTO: ESTATE OF PETER MOORE AND VAGA, NEW YORK

Below: Night Garden *installed at Bourgeois' exhibition at the Peridot Gallery, New York, 1953: "Louise Bourgeois: Drawings for Sculptures and Sculptures."*

1993
Bourgeois represents the United States at the American Pavilion of the Venice Biennale. She exhibits the first large-scale spider at the Brooklyn Museum. The City of Chicago, the Art Institue of Chicago, and Hull House select Bourgeois as the artist to make a sculpture park in honor of Jane Addams, the social and political activist who founded Hull House. Hull House is an educational institution for immigrants, particularly for women and children. She is presented with the "Mayor's Awards for Art and Culture" by the Mayor of New York City. Terra Luna Films and Centre Pompidou in Paris coproduce an hour-long documentary on Bourgeois, directed by Camille Guichard, for French television.

1994
Nigel Finch directs a one-hour documentary on Louise Bourgeois for Arena Films of the BBC in London.

1995
Bourgeois receives the "1995 Biennial Award" from the Royal Museum in Tokyo and the Hakone Open-Air Museum, Kanagawa-ken, Japan. She is also awarded an Honorary Doctorate of Fine Arts from the Art Institute of Chicago.

The French government commissions Bourgeois to create a sculpture in Choisy-le-Roi.

1997
Bourgeois is commissioned by the French government to make a large-scale work, *Toi et Moi*, in cast and polished aluminum for the new Bibliothèque Nationale de France in Paris, by architect Dominique Perrault. The "National Medal of Arts" is presented to Bourgeois by President Clinton at the White House.

1998
Bourgeois is commissioned by the Pittsburgh Cultural Trust to make a large-scale sculpture installation for Agnes R. Katz. The project is a collaboration with the architect Michael Graves and the landscape architect Dan Kiley.

1999
Bourgeois is awarded the Wexner Prize from the Wexner Center for the Arts at Ohio State University. Bourgeois receives the 1999 "Praemium Imperiale Award" in the sculpture category from the Japan Art Association.

2000
Bourgeois is commissioned for the inaugural installation at the new Tate Gallery of Modern Art. She conceives of a thirty-foot spider entitled *Maman* and three steel architectural towers employing the use of staircases and mirrors. The Fonds National d'Art Contemporain acquires *The Welcoming Hands,* a suite of six bronze hand poses mounted on granite, for permanent installation in the gardens of the Tuileries in Paris.

2001
The State Hermitage Museum in St. Petersburg mounts a Bourgeois retrospective, their first exhibition ever of a living American artist. Williams College in Williamstown, Massachusetts, commissions a large outdoor installation. Bourgeois celebrates her 90th birthday in New York City on December 25.

Bourgeois in 1966 inside her sculpture, The Blind Leading the Blind.

PHOTO: ESTATE OF PETER MOORE AND VAGA, NEW YORK

exhibitions

Louise Bourgeois' work has appeared in more than 200 solo exhibitions over the past seven decades. The following is a selection of both solo and group exhibitions. (Solo exhibitions are indicated by ✦✦.)

1936

- ✦ Galerie de Paris, Paris, France, "Exposition de l'Atelier de la Grande Chaumière," 1936.

1937

- ✦ 7, rue Joseph-Bara, Paris, France, "La Groupe 1938–1939 de l'Academie Ranson," 1937.

1940

- ✦ Brooklyn Museum of Art, Brooklyn, NY, "Fine Prints for Mass Production," 1940.

1942

- ✦ Metropolitan Museum of Art, New York, "Arts for Victory: An Exhibition of Painting, Sculpture and Graphic Arts," held under the auspices of Artists for Victory, Inc., 1942.

1943

- ✦ The Museum of Modern Art, New York, "The Arts in Therapy: A Competition and Exhibition" sponsored by The Museum of Modern Art in collaboration with Artists for Victory, Inc., 1943.

1944

- ✦ San Francisco Museum of Art, San Francisco, CA, and The Museum of Modern Art, New York, "Modern Drawings," 1944.
- ✦ Library of Congress, Washington, DC, "National Exhibition of Prints Made during the Current Year" ("The Pennell Show"), 1944.

1945

- ✦✦ Bertha Schaefer Gallery, New York, "Paintings by Louise Bourgeois," 1945.
- ✦ Whitney Museum of American Art, New York, "Annual Exhibition of Contemporary American Painting," 1945.
- ✦ Los Angeles County Museum of Art, Los Angeles, CA, "The First Biennial Exhibition of Drawings by American Artists," 1945.
- ✦ Art of This Century Gallery, New York, "The Women," 1945.
- ✦ Kurt Valentin Gallery, New York, and David Porter Gallery, Washington, DC, "Personal Statement: Painting Prophecy 1950"; traveled to Memorial Art Gallery, University of Rochester, 1945.
- ✦ The Museum of Modern Art, New York, "Textile Design," 1945.
- ✦ Buchholz Gallery, New York, "Contemporary Prints," 1945.

1946

- ✦ Whitney Museum of American Art, New York, "Annual Exhibition of Contemporary American Sculpture, Watercolors and Drawings," 1946.
- ✦ Bertha Schaefer Gallery, New York, "Directions in Abstraction," 1946.
- ✦ Bertha Schaefer Gallery, New York, "Flowers by Moderns," 1946.
- ✦ Bertha Schaefer Gallery, New York, "Watercolors, Temperas, Gouaches," 1946.
- ✦ Bertha Schaefer Gallery, New York, "The Horse in Painting and Sculpture," 1946.

1947

- ✦✦ Norlyst Gallery, New York, "Louise Bourgeois: Paintings," 1947.
- ✦ Bertha Schaefer Gallery, New York, "Fact and Fantasy," 1947.
- ✦ Wildenstein and Co., New York, "7th Annual Exhibition of Paintings and Sculpture by Guest Members of the Federation of Modern Painters and Sculptors," 1947.
- ✦ Norlyst Gallery, New York, "Seaboard and Midland Moderns" (national tour), 1947.
- ✦ Pennsylvania Academy of the Fine Arts and the Philadelphia Watercolor Club, Philadelphia, PA, "45th Annual Watercolor and Print Exhibition," 1947.
- ✦ Whitney Museum of American Art, New York, "Annual Exhibition of Contemporary American Painting," 1947.

1948

- ✦ Brooklyn Museum of Art, Brooklyn, "The Second Annual Exhibition of Contemporary American Painting," 1948.
- ✦ Whitney Museum of American Art, New York, "Annual Exhibition of Contemporary American Painting," 1948.

1949

- ✦✦ Peridot Gallery, New York, "Louise Bourgeois, Recent Work 1947–1949: Seventeen Standing Figures in Wood," 1949.
- ✦ The Museum of Modern Art, New York, "Master Prints from the Museum Collection," 1949.
- ✦ Laurel Gallery and Kende Galleries, New York, "Collection of Modern Art and Manuscripts Contributed to International Rescue, Inc.," 1949.
- ✦ The Brooklyn Museum of Art, Brooklyn, "Third Annual National Print Exhibition," 1949.
- ✦ Riverside Museum, New York, "13th Annual Exhibition of the American Abstract Artists," 1949.
- ✦ Peridot Gallery, New York, "Group Show," 1949.

1950

- ✦✦ Peridot Gallery, New York, "Louise Bourgeois: Sculptures," 1950.
- ✦ Peridot Gallery, New York, "The Year's Work," 1950.

1951

- ✦ The Museum of Modern Art, New York, "Recent Acquisitions," 1951.
- ✦ Whitney Museum of American Art, New York, "Annual Exhibition of Contemporary American Sculpture, Watercolors and Drawings," 1951.

1952

- ✦ Peridot Gallery, New York, "Group Show," 1952.
- ✦ Peridot Gallery, New York, "Recent Painting and Sculpture," 1952.

1953

- ✦✦ Peridot Gallery, New York, "Louise Bourgeois: Drawings for Sculpture and Sculpture," 1953.
- ✦ Allan Frumkin Gallery, Chicago, IL, 1953.
- ✦ Whitney Museum of American Art, New York, "Annual Exhibition of Contemporary American Sculpture, Watercolors and Drawings," 1953.
- ✦ Stable Gallery, New York, "Second Annual Exhibition of Paintings and Sculpture," 1953.
- ✦ Alan Frumkin Gallery, Chicago, IL, "Two Sculptors: Louise Bourgeois, Jeremy Anderson," 1953.
- ✦ Peridot Gallery, New York, "Watercolors, Collages, Drawings," 1953.
- ✦ Institute of Contemporary Art, Boston, MA, "40 Pictures from the Lee Ault Collection," 1953.
- ✦ Peridot Gallery, New York, "Watercolors and Drawings," 1953.
- ✦ Peridot Gallery, New York, "Group Show," 1953.

1954

- ✦ Walker Art Center, Minneapolis, MN, "Reality and Fantasy 1900–1954," 1954.
- ✦ Stable Gallery, New York, "Third Annual Exhibition of Painting and Sculpture," 1954.
- ✦ Riverside Museum, New York, "18th Annual Exhibition of American Abstract Artists," 1954.
- ✦ Whitney Museum of American Art, New York, "Annual Exhibition of Contemporary American Sculpture, Watercolors and Drawings," 1954.
- ✦ Private Residence, New York, "Sculpture in a Garden," 1954.

1955

- ✦ Whitney Museum of American Art, New York, "Annual Exhibition of Contemporary American Sculpture, Watercolors and Drawings," 1955.
- ✦ Krannert Art Museum, University of Illinois, Champaign, IL, "Contemporary American Painting and Sculpture," 1955.
- ✦ Poindexter Gallery, New York, "Drawings, Watercolors and Small Oils," 1955.
- ✦ Tanager Gallery, New York, "Sculpture Group," 1955.

1956

- ✦ Whitney Museum of American Art, New York, "Annual Exhibition of Contemporary American Sculpture, Watercolors and Drawings," 1956.
- ✦ Riverside Museum, New York, "20th Annual Exhibition of the American Abstract Artists," 1956.
- ✦ Stable Gallery, New York, "Fifth Annual Exhibition of Painting and Sculpture," 1956.

- ✦ Riverside Museum, New York, "16th Annual Exhibition of the Federation of Modern Painters and Sculptors," 1956.
- ✦ Whitney Museum of Contemporary Art, New York, "Annual Exhibition: Sculpture, Paintings, Watercolors, Drawings," 1956.
- ✦ Stable Gallery, New York, "Black and White," 1956.

1957

- ✦ Boston Public Garden, Boston, MA, "American Painting and Sculpture, 1957.
- ✦ "A National Invitational Exhibition" (Boston Arts Festival), 1957.
- ✦ Whitney Museum of American Art, New York, "Annual Exhibition of Contemporary American Sculpture, Watercolors and Drawings," 1957.

1958

- ✦ Allen Memorial Art Museum, Oberlin, OH, "Sculpture 1950–1958," 1958.
- ✦ Whitney Museum of American Art, New York, "Nature in Abstraction," 1958.

1959

- ✦✦ Andrew D. White Art Museum, Cornell University, Ithaca, "Sculpture by Louise Bourgeois" (one of five exhibitions that were part of a "Festival of Contemporary Arts"), 1959.

1960

- ✦ Dallas Museum of Contemporary Art, Dallas, TX, "To Be Continued: An Exhibition of the Museum Collection, Now and Prospect," 1960.
- ✦ Whitney Museum of Art, New York, "Annual Exhibition 1960: Contemporary Sculpture and Drawings," 1960.

1961

- ✦ The Museum of Modern Art, New York, "Recent Acquisitions," 1961.

1962

- ✦ Whitney Museum of American Art, New York, "Annual Exhibition 1962: Sculpture and Drawings," 1962.
- ✦ The Museum of Modern Art, New York, and Mount Holyoke College, South Hadley, MA, "Woman Artists in America Today," 1962.
- ✦ Tanager Gallery, New York, "The Closing Show: 1952–1962," 1962.

1963

- ✦ Whitney Museum of American Art, New York, and Washington Gallery of Modern Art, Washington, DC, "Treasures of 20th Century Art from the Maremont Collection," 1963.

1964

- ✦✦ Stable Gallery, New York, "Louise Bourgeois: Recent Sculpture," 1964.
- ✦ Rose Fried Gallery, New York, "Recent Drawings by Louise Bourgeois," 1964.

1965

- ✦ Musée Rodin, Paris, France, "XXVIIe Salon de la Jeune Sculpture," 1965.

1966

- ✦ Fischbach Gallery, New York, "Eccentric Abstraction," curated by Lucy Lippard, 1966.
- ✦ Museum of Art, Rhode Island School of Design, Providence, RI, "Recent Still Life," 1966.

1968

- ✦ Whitney Museum of American Art, New York, "Annual Exhibition: Sculpture," 1968.
- ✦ The American Federation of Arts, New York, "Soft Sculpture," organized by Lucy Lippard, 1968.

1969

- ✦ The Museum of Modern Art, New York, "The New American Painting and Sculpture: The First Generation," 1969.
- ✦ Baltimore Museum of Art, Baltimore, MD, "The Partial Figure in Modern Sculpture," 1969.

1970

- ✦ Museum of Art, Rhode Island School of Design, Providence, RI, "Governor's Arts Awards Exhibition," 1970.
- ✦ Whitney Museum of American Art, New York, "Annual Exhibition of Contemporary American Sculpture," 1970.

1972

✦ Women's Ad Hoc Committee at 117–119 Prince Street, New York, "13 Women Artists," 1972.

1973

✦ Whitney Museum of American Art, New York, "Biennial Exhibition: Contemporary American Art," 1973.

1974

✦✦ 112 Greene Street, New York, "Louise Bourgeois: Sculpture 1970–1974," 1974.

1975

✦ The Museum of Modern Art, New York, "American Art Since 1945 From the Collection of the Museum of Modern Art," 1975.

1976

✦ New Orleans Museum of Art, New Orleans, LA, "Sculpture: American Directions, 1945–1975," organized by the National Collection of Fine Arts, 1976.

✦ Whitney Museum of American Art, New York, "200 Years of American Sculpture," 1976.

1977

✦ Rose Art Museum, Brandeis University, Waltham, MA, "From Women's Eyes," 1977.

✦ Bronx Museum of the Arts, Bronx, "Images of Horror and Fantasy," 1977.

1978

✦✦ Hamilton Gallery of Contemporary Art, New York, "Louise Bourgeois: New Work"; includes a performance "A Banquet/A Fashion Show of Body Parts" in conjunction with the piece *Confrontation*, 1978.

✦✦ Xavier Fourcade Gallery, New York, "Louise Bourgeois: Triangles: New Sculpture and Drawings, 1978," 1978.

✦✦ University of California, Berkeley Art Museum, Berkeley, CA, "Louise Bourgeois: Matrix/Berkeley 17," 1978–1979.

1979

✦✦ Xavier Fourcade Gallery, New York, "Louise Bourgeois, Sculpture 1941–1953. Plus One New Piece," 1979.

1980

✦✦ Max Hutchinson Gallery, New York, "The Iconography of Louise Bourgeois" 1980.

✦✦ Xavier Fourcade Gallery, New York, "Louise Bourgeois Sculpture: The Middle Years 1955–1970," 1980.

✦ E. Lorenzo Borenstein Gallery, New Orleans, LA, "Women's Caucus for Art Honors: Albers, Bourgeois, Durieux, Kohlmeyer, Krasner," 1980.

1981

✦✦ Renaissance Society, University of Chicago, IL, "Louise Bourgeois: Femme Maison," 1981.

✦ Whitney Museum of American Art, New York, "Decade of Transition 1940–1950," 1981.

1982

✦✦ Robert Miller Gallery, New York, "Bourgeois Truth," 1982.

✦✦ The Museum of Modern Art, New York, "Louise Bourgeois: Retrospective"; traveled to Contemporary Arts Museum, Houston, TX ; Museum of Contemporary Art, Chicago, IL; Akron Art Museum, Akron, OH; 1982–1984.

✦ San Francisco Museum of Modern Art, San Francisco, CA, "Twenty American Artists: 1982 Sculpture," 1982.

1983

✦ Whitney Museum of American Art, New York, "1983 Whitney Museum Biennial Exhibition," 1983.

1984

✦ Whitney Museum of American Art, New York, "The Third Dimension: Sculpture of the New York School," 1984–1986.

✦ The Museum of Modern Art, New York, "Primitivism," 1984–1986.

1985

✦ Contemporary Arts Center, Cincinnati, OH, "Body and Soul: Aspects of Recent Figurative Sculpture," 1985.

✦ University of Pittsburgh Gallery, PA, "Sculpture by Women in the Eighties," 1985.

1986

✦✦ Texas Gallery, Houston, TX, "Louise Bourgeois: Sculptures and Drawings," 1986.

✦ Los Angeles Museum of Contemporary Art, Los Angeles, CA, "Individual: A Selected History of Contemporary Art, 1945–1986," 1986–1988.

1987

✦✦ Robert Miller Gallery, New York, "Louise Bourgeois: Paintings from the 1940s," 1987.

✦✦ Gallery Paule Anglim, San Francisco, CA, "Louise Bourgeois: Sculpture 1947–1955," 1987.

✦✦ The Taft Museum, Cincinnati, OH, "Louise Bourgeois"; traveled to The Art Museum at Florida International University, Miami, FL; Laguna Gloria Art Museum, Austin, TX; Gallery of Art, Washington University, St. Louis, MO; Everson Museum of Art, Syracuse, NY; 1987–1989.

✦ Whitney Museum of American Art, New York, Biennial, 1987.

1988

✦✦ Robert Miller Gallery, New York, "Louise Bourgeois: Drawings 1939–1987," 1988.

✦✦ Museum Overholland, Amsterdam, The Netherlands, "Louise Bourgeois: Works on Paper 1939–1988," 1988.

✦✦ Henry Art Gallery, University of Washington, Seattle, WA, "Louise Bourgeois: Works from 1943–1987," 1988–1989.

✦ Whitney Museum of American Art, New York, "Figure as Subject: The Revival of Figuration Since 1975"; traveled to Erwin A. Ulrich Museum of Art, Wichita State University, Wichita, KS; The Arkansas Arts Center, Little Rock, AR; Amarillo Art Center, Amarillo, TX; Utah Museum of Fine Arts, University of Utah, Salt Lake City, UT; and Madison Art Center, Madison, WI, 1988–1989.

1989

✦✦ Dia Art Foundation, Bridgehampton, "Louise Bourgeois: Works from the Sixties," 1989.

✦✦ Ydessa Hendeles Art Foundation, Toronto, Canada, "Louise Bourgeois: Legs," 1989–1990.

✦✦ Frankfurter Kunstverein, Frankfurt, West Germany, "Louise Bourgeois: A Retrospective Exhibition"; traveled to Stadtische Galerie im Lenbachhaus, Munich, West Germany; Musée d'Art Contemporain, Lyon, France; Fondacion Tapies, Barcelona, Spain; Kunstmuseum, Bern, Switzerland; and Kröller-Muller Museum, Otterlo, The Netherlands; 1989–1991.

✦ Museum Ludwig, Cologne, West Germany, "Bilderstreit," 1989.

✦ Cincinnati Art Museum, Eden Park, OH, "Making Their Mark: Woman Artists Move into the Mainstream 1970–1985"; traveled to New Orleans Museum of Art, New Orleans; Denver Art Museum, Denver, CO; Pennsylvania Academy of the Fine Arts, Philadelphia, PA, 1989–1990.

1990

✦✦ Riverside Studios, London, England, "Louise Bourgeois: 1984–1989," 1990.

✦✦ The Ginny Williams Gallery, Denver, CO, "Bourgeois Four Decades," 1990.

✦ Wexner Center for the Visual Arts, The Ohio State University, Columbus, OH, "Inaugural Exhibition Part II—Art in Europe and America: The 1960s and 1970s," 1990.

✦ Museum of Fine Arts, Boston, MA, "Figuring the Body," 1990.

✦ Museum Wiesbaden, Wiesbaden, Germany, "Positions of Art in the 20th Century: 50 Woman Artists," 1990.

1991

✦✦ Ydessa Hendeles Art Foundation, Toronto, Canada, "Louise Bourgeois," 1991.

✦ The Museum of Modern Art, New York, "Art of the Forties," 1991.

✦ The Hudson River Museum, Yonkers, "Experiencing Sculpture: The Figurative Presence in America, 1870–1990," 1991–1992.

✦ The Carnegie Museum of Art, Pittsburgh, PA, "Carnegie International," 1991–1992.

✦ The Museum of Modern Art, New York, "Dislocations," 1991–1992.

1992

- ✦✦ Milwaukee Art Museum, Milwaukee, WI, "Currents 21: Louise Bourgeois," 1992.
- ✦✦ National Gallery of Art, Washington, DC, installation of recent acquisitions, East Wing, 1992–1993.
- ✦ Kassel, Germany, "Documenta IX," 1992.
- ✦ Solomon R. Guggenheim Museum, New York, "Masterpieces From the Guggenheim Collection," 1992.
- ✦ Guggenheim Museum Soho, New York, "From Brancusi to Bourgeois: Aspects of the Guggenheim Collection," 1992.
- ✦ List Visual Arts Center, Massachusetts Institute of Technology, Cambridge, MA, "Corporal Politics," 1992–1993.

1993

- ✦✦ Ginny Williams Family Foundation, Denver, CO, "Louise Bourgeois," 1993–1994.
- ✦✦ American Pavilion, Venice Biennale, Venice, Italy; with an expanded exhibition "Louise Bourgeois: The Locus of Memory"; traveled to the Brooklyn Museum of Art, Brooklyn, NY; The Corcoran Gallery of Art, Washington, DC; Galerie Rudolfinum, Prague, Czech Republic; Musée d'Art Moderne de la Ville de Paris, Paris, France; Deichtorhallen, Hamburg, Germany; Musée d'Art Contemporain de Montreal, Montreal, Canada, 1993–1996.
- ✦ Art Contemporain, Lyon, France, "Here's Looking At Me: Contemporary Self Portrait," 1993.

1994

- ✦✦ Galerie Karsten Greve, Cologne, Germany, "Louise Bourgeois: Drawings and Early Sculptures, Sculptures and Installations," 1994.
- ✦✦ The Saint Louis Art Museum, St. Louis, MO, "Louise Bourgeois: The Personages," 1994.
- ✦✦ Nelson-Atkins Museum of Art, Kansas City, MO, "Louise Bourgeois," 1994.
- ✦✦ Kestner-Gesellschaft, Hannover, Germany, "Louise Bourgeois: Sculptures," 1994.
- ✦✦ Peter Blum Gallery, New York, "Louise Bourgeois: The Red Rooms," 1994.
- ✦✦ Archives of American Art, New York, "The Louise Bourgeois Papers: A Promised Gift to the Archives of American Art," 1994.
- ✦✦ The Museum of Modern Art, New York, "Louise Bourgeois: Print Retrospective"; traveled to the Bibliotheque Nationale, Paris, France; Musée du Dessin et de l'Estampe Originale, Gravelines, France; The Museum of Modern Art, Oxford, England; Bonnefanten Museum, Maastricht, The Netherlands; 1994–1996.
- ✦ Tampa Museum of Art, Tampa, FL, "Between Transcendence and Brutality: American Sculptural Drawings from the 1940s and 1950s"; traveled to Arkansas Art Center, Little Rock, AR, and The Parrish Art Museum, Southhampton, 1994.
- ✦ The Irish Museum of Modern Art, Dublin, Ireland, "From Beyond the Pale," 1994–1995.

1995

- ✦✦ L'Ecole Nationale de Beaux Arts de Bourges, Bourges, France, "Louise Bourgeois: Drawings," 1995.
- ✦✦ Musée National d'Art Moderne, Centre Georges Pompidou, Paris, France, "Louise Bourgeois: Pensées-plumes"; traveled to Helsinki City Art Museum, Helsinki, Finland; 1995.
- ✦✦ MARCO, Monterrey, Mexico, "Louise Bourgeois"; traveled to Centro Andaluz de Arte Contemporaneo, Seville, Spain; Museo Rufino Tamayo, Mexico City, Mexico; 1995–1996.
- ✦ Venice Biennale, Venice, Italy, "XLVI Esposizione Internationale d'Arte," 1995.
- ✦ The Tate Gallery, London, England, "Rites of Passage," 1995.
- ✦ Museum of Contemporary Art, Tokyo, Japan, "Revolution in Contemporary Art: The Art of the Sixties," 1995.
- ✦ Centre Georges Pompidou, Paris, France, "Feminin-Masculin: Le Sexe de l'Art," 1995–1996.

1996

- ✦✦ Berkeley Art Museum, University of California, Berkeley, CA, "Louise Bourgeois: Drawings"; traveled to The Drawing Center, New York; The List

Visual Art Center, Massachusetts Institute of Technology, Boston, MA; 1996.

✦✦ Rupertinum, Salzburg, Austria, "Louise Bourgeois: Sculptures and Objects," 1996.

✦✦ Gallery Joseloff, Harry Jack Gray Center, University of Hartford, West Hartford, CT, "Louise Bourgeois: The Forties and Fifties," 1996.

✦✦ Galerie Hauser and Wirth, Zurich, Switzerland, "Louise Bourgeois: Red Room Installation / Drawings," 1996–1997.

✦✦ Galerie Soledad Lorenzo, Madrid, Spain, "Louise Bourgeois," 1996–1997.

✦✦ Xavier Hufkens Gallery, Brussels, Belgium, "Louise Bourgeois," 1996–1997.

✦ The Institute of Contemporary Art, Boston, MA, "Inside the Visible"; traveled to National Museum of Women in the Arts, 1996.

✦ Musée d'Art Moderne de la Ville de Paris, France, "Passions Privées," 1996.

✦ 23rd International Sao Paulo Bienal, "Louise Bourgeois," Sao Paulo, Brazil, designed exhibition posters, 1996.

✦ St. Pancras Church, London, England, "The Visible & The Invisible: Re-presenting the Body in Contemporary Art and Society" organized by Institute of International Visual Arts, 1996.

1997

✦✦ Cheim & Read, New York, "Louise Bourgeois: Spider," 1997.

✦✦ The Contemporary Arts Center, Cincinnati, OH, "Louise Bourgeois: Ode à Ma Mère," 1997.

✦✦ Prada Foundation, Milan, Italy, "Louise Bourgeois: Blue Days and Pink Days," 1997.

✦ Guggenheim Museum Soho, New York, "Art / Fashion," 1997.

✦ Whitney Museum of American Art, New York, "1997 Whitney Museum Biennial Exhibition," 1997.

✦ Maison de Lyon, Lyon, France, "Biennale d'Art Contemporain de Lyon," 1997.

1998

✦✦ Yokohama Museum of Art, Yokohama, Japan, "Louise Bourgeois: Homesickness," 1997–1998.

✦✦ The Arts Club of Chicago, IL, "Louise Bourgeois," 1997–1998.

1998

✦✦ North Carolina Museum of Art, Raleigh, NC, "Sacred and Fatal: The Art of Louise Bourgeois," 1998.

✦✦ Whitney Museum of American Art, New York, "Louise Bourgeois: Topiary," 1998.

✦✦ The Art Gallery of Ontario, Toronto, Canada, "Present Tense: Louise Bourgeois," 1998.

✦✦ Musee d'Art Contemporain, Bordeaux, France, "Louise Bourgeois"; traveled to Foundation Belem, Lisbon, Portugal; Malmö Konsthall, Malmö, Sweden; Serpentine Gallery, London, England; 1998–1999.

✦ The First Ladies Garden, The White House, Washington, DC, "Twentieth Century Sculpture: Inspired by Rodin," 1998.

✦ XXIV Bienal de Sao Paulo, Sao Paulo, Brazil, "Cannibalism," 1998.

✦ Kunsthalle Wien, Vienna, Austria, "Bourgeois-Holzer-Lang," 1998–2000.

✦ Taipei Fine Arts Museum, Taiwan, Republic of China, "Les Champs de la Sculpture," 1998–2000.

1999

✦✦ Galerie Karsten Greve, Cologne, Germany, "Louise Bourgeois," 1999.

✦✦ Kunsthalle Bielefeld, Bielefeld, Germany, "Louise Bourgeois," 1999.

✦✦ Wexner Center for the Visual Arts, Columbus, OH, "Wexner Prize Wall," 1999.

✦✦ Museo Nacional Centro de Arte—Reina Sofia, Madrid, Spain, "Louise Bourgeois: Architecture and Memory," 1999–2000.

✦ The Israel Museum, Jerusalem, Israel, "Skin-Deep: Surface and Appearance in Contemporary Art," 1999.

✦ 48th International Exhibition of Contemporary Art, La Biennale di Venezia, Venice, Italy.

✦ California College of Arts and Crafts, Oakland, CA, "Searchlight: Consciousness at the Millennium," 1999.

✦ Whitney Museum of American Art, New York, "The American Century: Art and Culture, 1950–2000," 1999.

- ✦ Museum Ludwig, Cologne, Germany, "Artworlds in Dialogue," 1999.
- ✦ Hirshhorn Museum and Sculpture Garden, Washington, DC, "Regarding Beauty: A View of the Late Twentieth Century," traveled to Haus der Kunst, Munich, Germany, 1999.
- ✦ Reina Sofia / Museo Nacional Centro de Arte, Madrid, Spain, "Surrealists in Exile and the Beginning of the New York School"; traveled to the Musée d'Art Moderne et Contemporain, Strasbourg, Austria, 1999.

2000

- ✦✦ Tate Modern, London, England, "Louise Bourgeois: Inaugural Installation of the Tate Modern Art at Turbine Hall," 2000.
- ✦✦ National Museum of Contemporary Art, Kyunggi-Do, Korea, "Louise Bourgeois: The Space of Memory," 2000.
- ✦✦ Tate Modern, London, England, "Louise Bourgeois: The Insomnia Drawings," 2000–2001.
- ✦ Cheim & Read, New York, "Couples," 2000.
- ✦ Museum Boijmans Van Beuningen, Rotterdam, The Netherlands, "Exorcism/Aesthetic Terrorism," 2000.
- ✦ The National Gallery, London, England, "Encounters—New Art from Old," 2000.
- ✦ Sammlung Hauser und Wirth, St. Gallen, Switzerland, "The Oldest Possible Memory," 2000.

2001

- ✦✦ C&M Arts, New York, "Louise Bourgeois: The Personages," 2001.
- ✦✦ The State Hermitage Museum, St. Petersburg, Russia, "Louise Bourgeois at the Hermitage"; traveled to Helsinki City Art Museum, Helsinki, Finland; Kulturhuset, Stockholm, Sweden; Museet for Samtidskunst, Oslo, Norway, 2001–2002.
- ✦✦ Guggenheim Museum Bilbao, Bilbao, Spain, "Louise Bourgeois," 2001–2002.
- ✦✦ Cheim & Read, New York, "Louise Bourgeois: New Work," 2001–2002.
- ✦✦ Williams College Museum of Art, Williamstown, MA, "Louise Bourgeois: Sleepwalking," 2001–2002.
- ✦ Xavier Hufkens Gallery, Brussels, "Richard Artschwager, Louise Bourgeois, Roni Horn, Allan McCollum," 2001.
- ✦ Staatsgalerie Stuttgart, Stuttgart, Germany, "Rodin to Baselitz: The Torso in Modern Sculpture," 2001.
- ✦ Kunstmuseum Bern, Bern, Switzerland, "Black Box: The Dark Room in Art," 2001.
- ✦ Cheim & Read, New York, "Liquid Properties," 2001.
- ✦ Tate Modern, London, England, "Surrealism: Desire Unbound"; traveled to Metropolitan Museum of Art, New York, 2001–2002.

2002

- ✦✦ Krannert Art Museum, University of Illinois, Champaign, IL, "Louise Bourgeois: The Early Work"; traveled to Madison Art Center, Madison, WI; Aspen Art Museum, Aspen, CO; 2002–2003.
- ✦✦ Galerie Hauser & Wirth, Zurich, Switzerland, "Louise Bourgeois: Marbles," 2002.

bibliography

The following bibliography includes a selected list of books and a complete list of periodicals up to 1970. Periodicals published after that date have not been included.

1945

Devree, Howard. "Exhibition review, Bertha Schaefer Gallery." *The New York Times*, June 10, 1945, Sec. II, 2.

———. "Exhibition review, Bertha Schaefer Gallery." *New York Herald Tribune*, June 10, 1945.

Porter, David, ed. *Natural History in Personal Statement* (exhibition catalogue). Washington: David Porter Gallery, 1945.

R(eed), J(udith) K. "Exhibition review, Bertha Schaefer Gallery." *Art Digest* 19 (June 1945): 31.

———. "Exhibition review, Bertha Schaefer Gallery." *Artnews* 44 (June 1945): 30, 37.

1947

R(eed), J(udith) K. "Exhibition review, Norlyst Gallery." *New York Sun*, October 31, 1947.

———. "Exhibition review, Norlyst Gallery." *The New York Times*, November 2, 1947.

———. "Exhibition review, Norlyst Gallery." *Artnews* 46, no. 9 (November 1947): 42.

1948

"Artists." *Magazine of Art* 41 (December 1948): 307.

1949

Bewley, Marius. "An Introduction to Louise Bourgeois." *The Tiger's Eye* 1, no. 7 (March 15, 1949): 89-92.

Preston, Stuart. "Exhibition review, Peridot Gallery." *The New York Times*, October 9, 1949, Sect. II, 9.

———. "Exhibition review, Peridot Gallery." *New York Sun*, October 14, 1949.

S(harp), M(arynell). "Telegraphic Constructions." *Art Digest* 24 (October 15, 1949): 22.

The Tiger's Eye 9 (October 15, 1949): 52.

M.C. "Debut as Sculptor at Peridot." *Artnews* 48, no. 6 (October 1949): 46.

1950

L(evy), P(esella). "Exhibition review, Peridot Gallery." *Art Digest* 25 (October 1, 1950): 16.

Preston, Stuart. "'Primitive' to Abstraction in Current Shows." *The New York Times*, October 8, 1950, Sec. II, 9.

R.C. "Exhibition review, Peridot Gallery." *Artnews* 49, no. 6 (October 1950): 48.

1951

Motherwell, Robert, and Ad Reinhardt, texts. In *Modern Artists in America*, 8–22, 86, 100, 133. New York: Wittenborn Schultz, 1951.

1952

Fitzsimmons, James. "Recent Painting and Sculpture, Peridot Gallery." *Art Digest* 26, no. 15 (May 1, 1952).

1953

G(eist), S(idney). "Louise Bourgeois." *Art Digest* 27 (April 1, 1953): 17.

Fitzsimmons, James. "Exhibition review, Peridot Gallery." *Arts and Architecture* 70 (April 1953): 35.

P(orter), F(airfield), "Exhibition review, Peridot Gallery." *Artnews* 52 (April 1953).

Krasne, Belle. "10 Artists in the Margin." *Design Quarterly* 30 (1954): 9–22.

1956

Munro, Eleanor. "Explorations in Form." *Perspectives USA* 16 (Summer 1956): 160–72.

Goldwater, Robert. "La Sculpture Actuelle à New York." *Cimaise* 4 (November–December 1956): 24–28.

Hess, Thomas B. "Mutt Furioso." *Artnews* 55 (December 1956): 22–25, 64–65.

M. J.R. "Whitney Annual." *Arts* 31 (December 1956): 52.

1958

Hess, Thomas B. "Inside Nature." *Artnews* 56 (February 1958): 63.

———. "Sculpture 1950–58." *Oberlin College Bulletin*, New York, NY, vol. 15, no. 2 (Winter 1958): 66.

1959

Berckelaers, F.L. "Le Choix d'un critique." *Oeil* 49 (January 1959): 28, 30.

Ragon, Michel. "L'Art actuel aux Etas-Unis: Art Today in the United States." *Cimaise* (January–March 1959): 6–35.

1961

Pearlstein, Philip. "The Private Myth." *Artnews* 60 (September 1961): 42–45, 62.

1962

Oeri, Georgine. "A Propos of 'The Figure.'" *Quadrum: Revue Internationale d'Art Moderne* 13 (1962): 49–60.

1964

Oeri, Georgine. "Exhibition review, Stable Gallery." *Herald-Tribune*, London, January 11, 1964.

Preston, Stuart. "Exhibition review, Stable Gallery." *New York Times*, January 19, 1964, 23.

Oeri, Georgine. "Exhibition review, Stable and Fried Galleries." *New York Post*, January 26, 1964.

E(dgar), N(atalie). "Exhibition review, Stable Gallery." *Artnews* 62 (January 1964): 10.

R. V. "Exhibition review, Stable Gallery." *Arts* 38 (March 1964): 63.

Robbins, Daniel. "Sculpture by Louise Bourgeois." *Art International*, Paris, 8 (October 20, 1964): 29–31.

1965

Robbins, Daniel. "Waldorf Panels 1 and 2 on Sculpture." *It Is* 6 (Autumn 1965): 12, 30, 54, 71, 123.

1966

Robbins, Daniel. "Recent Still Life." *Art in America* 54 (January-February 1966): 57–60.

Lippard, Lucy R. "Eccentric Abstraction." *Art International* 10 (November 20, 1966): 28, 34–40.

Antin, David. "Another Category: 'Eccentric Abstraction.'" *Artforum* 5 (November 1966): 56, 57.

Ashton, Dore. "Marketing Techniques in the Promotion of Art." *Studio International*, London, vol. 172, no. 883 (November 1966): 270–73.

B(ochner), M(el). "Eccentric Abstraction." *Arts* 41 (November 1966): 58.

1967

Andersen, Wayne. "American Sculpture: The Situation in the Fifties." *Artforum* 5 (Summer 1967): 60–67.

1968

Ashton, Dore. *Modern American Sculpture*. New York: Abrams, 1968.

1969

Bourgeois, Louise. "Fabric of Construction at MoMA." *Craft Horizons* 29 (March–April 1969): 30–35.

Elsen, Albert, intro. *The Partial Figure in Modern Sculpture* (exhibition catalogue). Baltimore: Baltimore Museum of Art, 1969.

———. "Notes on the Partial Figure." *Artforum* 8 (November 1969): 58–63.

Goldwater, Robert. *What is Modern Sculpture?*. New York: The Museum of Modern Art, 1969.

Rubin, William. "Some Reflections Prompted by the Recent Work of Louise Bourgeois." *Art International* 8 (April 1969): 17–20.

———. "Louise Bourgeois." *Art Now* 1, no. 7 (September 1969).

1970

Ashton, Dore, intro. *L'Art vivant aux Etats-Unis*. St. Paul de Vence, France: Foundation Maeght, 1970.

———, text for entry of Louise Bourgeois. *The Britannica Encyclopedia of American Art*, 79. Chicago: Encyclopedia Britannica Educational Corporation, 1973.

1976

Krauss, Rosalind E. "Magician's Game: Decades of Transformation." In *200 Years of American Sculpture*, 168, 173, 176, and 191. New York: Whitney Museum of American Art and Boston: David R. Godine, 1976.

Lippard, Lucy R. "Louise Bourgeois: From the Inside Out." In *From the Center: Feminist Essays on Women's Art*, 238–249. New York: E. P. Dutton, 1976.

1977

Krauss, Rosalind E. *Passages in Modern Sculpture*, 148, 151. New York: Viking, 1977.

Wye, Deborah. "Louise Bourgeois." In *From Women's Eyes* (exhibition catalogue), 14–19. Waltham, MA: Rose Art Museum, Brandeis University, 1977.

1980

Gorovoy, Jerry. *The Iconography of Louise Bourgeois* (exhibition catalogue). New York: Max Hutchinson Gallery, 1980.

1982

Pincus-Whitten, Robert. *Bourgeois Truth* (exhibition catalogue). New York: Robert Miller Gallery, 1982.

Wye, Deborah. *Louise Bourgeois* (exhibition catalogue for her retrospective). New York: The Museum of Modern Art, 1982.

1983

Hanhardt, John G., with Barbara Haskell, Richard Marshall, and Patterson Sims. *1983 Biennial Exhibition* (exhibition catalogue). New York: Whitney Museum of American Art, 1983.

Lippard, Lucy R. "Homes and Graves and Gardens." In *Overlay Contemporary Art and The Art of Prehistory*. Pantheon Books, 1983.

Phillips, Lisa. *Twentieth Century Sculpture: Process and Presence* (exhibition catalogue). New York: Whitney Museum of American Art at Phillip Morris, 1983.

1984

Phillips, Lisa. *The Third Dimension: Sculpture of the New York School*. New York: Whitney Museum of American Art, 1984.

1985

Sischy, Ingrid. *Forms in Wood: American Sculpture of the 1950s* (exhibition catalogue). Philadelphia: Philadelphia Art Alliance, 1985.

Szeemann, Harald. *Spuren Skulpturen und Monumente ihrer präzisen Reise* (exhibition catalogue). Zurich: Kunsthaus, 1985–1986.

1986

Gorovoy, Jerry. *Louise Bourgeois* (exhibition catalogue). New York: Robert Miller Gallery, 1986.

1987

Morgan, Stuart. *Louise Bourgeois* (exhibition catalogue). Cincinnati, OH: The Taft Museum, 1987.

1988

Beckett, Wendy. *Contemporary Women Artists*. Oxford: Phaidon Press, 1988.

Cheim, John, and Jerry Gorovoy, eds., with introduction by Robert Storr. *Louise Bourgeois Drawings*. New York: Robert Miller Gallery and Paris: Daniel Lelong, 1988.

Kuspit, Donald. *Bourgeois* (an interview with Louise Bourgeois). New York: Elizabeth Avedon Editions/ Vintage Contemporary Artists, 1988.

1989

Geldzahler, Henry. *Louise Bourgeois* (exhibition catalogue). Bridgehampton, NY: Dia Art Foundation, 1989.

Weiermair, Peter, with Lucy Lippard, Rosalind Krauss et.al. *Louise Bourgeois* (European retrospective catalogue). Frankfurt: Frankfurter Kunstverein, 1989. English-language reprint, 1995.

1990

Morgan, Stuart. *Louise Bourgeois: Recent Work 1984–1989* (exhibition catalogue). London: Riverside Studios, 1990.

1991

Cooke, Lynne and Mark Francis. *Carnegie International 1991*. New York: Rizzoli, and Pittsburgh: The Carnegie Museum of Art, (volumes I and II), 1991.

Storr, Robert. *Devil on the Stairs* (exhibition catalogue). Philadelphia: Institute of Contemporary Art, University of Pennsylvania, 1991.

———. *Dislocations* (exhibition catalogue). New York: The Museum of Modern Art, 1991.

1992

Meyer-Thoss, Christiane. *Louise Bourgeois: Designing For Free Fall*. Zurich: Ammann Verlag, 1992.

Miller, Arthur, and Louise Bourgeois. *Homely Girl, A Life*. New York: Peter Blum Edition, 1992.

1993

Kotik, Charlotta. *Louise Bourgeois Recent Work* (exhibition brochure for United States Pavilion). Published by the United States Information Agency with copyright by The Brooklyn Museum, New York, 1993.

1994

Fineberg, Jonathan. *Art Since 1940: Strategies of Being*. Englewood Cliffs, NJ: Prentice-Hall, 1994.

Gardner, Paul. *Louise Bourgeois*. New York: Universe Publishing, 1994.